THE GLASS CASTLE

Jeannette Walls

*sparknotes

SPARKNOTES and the distinctive SparkNotes logo
are registered trademarks of SparkNotes LLC.

© 2020 SparkNotes LLC

This 2020 edition printed for SparkNotes LLC
by Sterling Publishing Co., Inc.

ISBN 978-1-4114-8036-0

Distributed in Canada by Sterling Publishing Co., Inc.
c/o Canadian Manda Group, 664 Annette Street
Toronto, Ontario M6S 2C8, Canada
Distributed in the United Kingdom by GMC Distribution Services
Castle Place, 166 High Street, Lewes, East Sussex BN7 1XU, England
Distributed in Australia by NewSouth Books
University of New South Wales, Sydney, NSW 2052, Australia

For information about custom editions, special sales, and premium
and corporate purchases, please contact Sterling Special Sales at
800-805-5489 or specialsales@sterlingpublishing.com.

Manufactured in Canada

Lot #:
2 4 6 8 10 9 7 5 3 1
09/20

sparknotes.com
sterlingpublishing.com

Please email content@sparknotes.com to report any errors.

CONTENTS

CONTEXT

Jeannette Walls was born in Phoenix, Arizona, in 1960. As a child, her family moved all over the American Southwest. They had very little money and routinely experienced hunger and homelessness. Jeannette's mother, Rose Mary Walls, was a passionate painter and ambivalent about cooking meals and cleaning the house. Her father, Rex Walls, suffered from severe alcoholism. For the most part, her parents took a laissez-faire approach to parenting, which meant that Jeannette and her siblings—Lori, Brian, and Maureen—were often left to protect and feed themselves. When Jeannette was a teenager, the family moved to Rex's Appalachian hometown of Welch, West Virginia. There, Jeannette started working at the school newspaper, the *Maroon Wave*, in the seventh grade because it was the only club that didn't require money to join. This experience launched her lifelong interest in journalism. At seventeen, Jeannette followed her sister Lori to New York City, where she finished high school and interned at a Brooklyn newspaper called *The Phoenix*. After graduating high school, she put herself through Barnard College with grants, loans, scholarships, and part-time work. Jeannette graduated with honors in 1984.

After college, Jeannette worked first as a reporter for *New York* magazine, and then as a gossip columnist for MSNBC.com, sometimes using tips from her father. During this phase of her career, Jeannette wrote a particularly negative article that targeted the Church of Scientology. The Church retaliated by investigating Walls's parents and threatened to expose her unconventional history. At this point, Jeannette's parents lived as squatters in Manhattan's Lower East Side, and often appeared on the local news, talking about squatters' rights. Although she remained in close contact with her parents, Jeannette worried she would lose her job and connections if people knew the truth about her past. She had hoped to keep the details of her life a secret. However, her husband, John, thought her life would make a great book. He encouraged her to tell her story on her own terms rather than risk cruel exposure, and this became the impetus for writing *The Glass Castle*.

Although Rex's reckless behavior caused most of the Walls family's upheaval, the exploitative business practices of the mining companies Rex found work with exacerbated their financial troubles. Throughout the early to mid-twentieth century, mining companies would build camps—also known as company towns—to provide the amenities that miners and their families needed to survive. Because the companies owned every establishment in the area, they controlled both the miners' wages and their cost of living. Companies often abused this arrangement, adjusting prices and wages to drive miners into debt, and essentially making them indentured servants. The remote nature of many of these camps meant that miners had no access to other stores or the freedom to seek other jobs. For many industries, the practice of creating company towns had largely fallen out of favor by the 1930s thanks to President Franklin D. Roosevelt's New Deal. However, many of the mining communities the Walls family lived in or around still operated in a similar way.

The Walls family arrived in Welch in the early 1970s, a time of heightened racial tension in the United States. During the Civil Rights Movement of the 1950s and 60s, black activists engaged in public protest and civil disobedience to demand that the federal government uphold their civil rights and bring an end to racially segregated public spaces. White resentment grew as black Americans gained the constitutional and legal rights that white Americans had long enjoyed. In more impoverished communities like Welch, this resentment often manifested as blame. On April 4, 1968, in Memphis, Tennessee, a white man named James Earl Ray assassinated Martin Luther King Jr. King's assassination led many black activists to feel that white America considered even nonviolent action too threatening. Throughout *The Glass Castle*, Jeannette encounters both suspicion from black neighbors and horrific vitriolic racism of white neighbors.

Walls published *The Glass Castle* in 2005 to much critical and popular acclaim. The book remained on *The New York Times* Best Seller list for years, and in 2017 was made into a movie, starring Brie Larson as Jeannette. Walls has since published two more full-length books, *Half-Broke Horses* and *Silver Star*. Walls lives with her husband John on a 205-acre farm in Virginia. Rose Mary lives in a cottage on Jeannette's farm, where she still paints and collects art. Rex died of a heart attack in New York City in 1994. Despite her father's reckless alcoholism, Jeannette cherishes the relationship she had with him. Compared to her mother and siblings, Jeannette was the most enthusiastic advocate of her father's wild antics and extravagant aspirations, extending him grace and compassion when the rest of the family couldn't. To this day, Walls credits her self-confidence to their special bond, saying he instilled in her the courage, gratitude, and intelligence she needed to be happy in life. She doesn't see herself as a victim of child abuse, but rather an exemplary product of alternative parenting.

CONTEXT

PLOT OVERVIEW

Jeannette Walls begins her memoir with a scene from adulthood. While in a taxicab in New York City, Jeannette looks out the window and sees her mother dumpster diving. She ducks down in her seat to avoid being recognized, but later invites her mother to lunch to talk about how she can help. Mom insists that she and Dad like being homeless and admonishes Jeannette for being ashamed of her own family. From here, Jeannette's narration goes back in time to her very first memory. At three years old, Jeannette lives in a trailer park with Mom, Dad, her older sister Lori, and her little brother Brian. Jeannette's tutu catches fire while she cooks hot dogs over a stove, and her mother rushes her to the hospital for an emergency skin graft. After six weeks in the hospital, Dad smuggles her out without paying the bill. Back at home, Jeannette continues cooking unsupervised and starts playing with matches.

One night, Dad makes the family pack all their belongings into the family car and move in the middle of the night, a routine he calls "doing the skedaddle." Over the next several years, the Wallses do the skedaddle dozens of times, moving all over to stay ahead of debt collectors and law enforcement. They spend a month or two in larger cities like Las Vegas and San Francisco, where Dad can make quick money by gambling. Most of the time, however, the Wallses live in isolated desert mining towns, where Mom and Dad teach their children reading and math, as well as specialized survival skills. Dad drinks often and struggles to keep a job, but he promises his family that their nomadic lifestyle is temporary. He promises to find gold and build his family the Glass Castle, a large, self-sustaining home made out of glass.

When Jeannette is in the first grade, Mom gives birth to another baby, Maureen. Dad moves the family to Battle Mountain, Nevada, where he works as an electrician. The family enjoys six months of relative stability until Dad loses his job. After an explosive argument, Mom gets a teaching job. Dad confiscates most of her paycheck, and the family continues to go hungry. Their time in Nevada comes to an end when Billy Deel, a delinquent neighbor boy whose advances Jeannette rejected, comes to the Walls residence and opens fire with his BB gun. Jeannette returns fire with Dad's pistol. She misses him on purpose, but the police get involved. The family flees to Phoenix. On the way to Phoenix, Jeannette learns that Grandma Smith has died, leaving Mom a large sum of money and a house. They move into Grandma's massive house, and Dad gets a job as an electrician. For about a year, the kids enjoy regular meals, their own bicycles, and public schooling. Unfortunately, Dad loses his job, and his alcoholism reaches crushing lows. The family is once again destitute. Mom decides it's time to move to Dad's hometown of Welch, West Virginia.

When the Wallses arrive in Welch, they stay with Jeannette's paternal grandmother, Erma. Erma is a bitter, unwelcoming host, and most people in Welch regard the Wallses as self-important outsiders. When Mom and Dad leave for an extended road trip to Phoenix, Erma molests Brian. Jeannette and Lori confront her, but Erma retaliates violently. Dad takes Erma's side when he returns, but Erma evicts the family. The Wallses buy a small rotting house with no running water or indoor plumbing. Dad admits that the conditions are not ideal but promises to use the land to begin construction on the Glass Castle. To help Dad get started on the Glass Castle, Brian and Jeannette dig a large hole for the foundation, but the family soon fills it with garbage. To survive, the kids start dumpster diving and stealing food from their classmates and neighbors. Desperate, Jeannette begs Mom to divorce Dad so they can go on welfare, but Mom refuses.

When the Wallses get a visit from child protective services, Mom finds a teaching job. The money could solve their problems, but Dad's extensive drinking once again drains their funds, and the family continues to go hungry. The following summer, Mom goes to Charleston for several weeks to renew her teaching license. Left in control of the family finances, Jeannette finds that she, too, gives in to Dad's demands for more money. When Mom returns from Charleston, she announces that she will quit her job and devote all her time to art. Jeannette finally confronts Mom and Dad about their selfishness, but Dad whips her in retaliation. Appalled, Jeannette and Lori plan to move to New York City as soon as possible. Jeannette, Lori, and Brian find jobs around Welch and save all their money for almost a year, but Dad steals the money just months before Lori's planned departure. In the end, Jeannette secures Lori a summer babysitting job that includes a bus ticket to New York City as payment.

Lori loves life in New York City, where she works in a restaurant and lives in a women's hostel. Jeannette moves to the city a year later and finishes high school there, interning at a Brooklyn newspaper for credit. Brian follows a year later. Jeannette starts college at Barnard, putting herself through with grants, loans, and savings from odd jobs. Maureen moves in with Lori at age twelve. Dad accuses Lori of stealing his children, and he and Mom move to New York City three years later. After being kicked out of several apartments, Mom and Dad first live on the streets, and then become squatters. At this point, Jeannette has married and works at a prestigious magazine. Lori is an artist, and Brian is a police officer. Maureen drops out of college and moves in with Mom and Dad. Maureen tries to stab Mom and must spend a year in a psychiatric hospital. The family drifts apart, and a year later Dad dies of a heart attack. Five years after Dad's death, Jeannette and her second husband, John, host the family for Thanksgiving, though without Maureen. They toast to Dad's life.

Character List

Jeannette Walls   The protagonist and narrator of the memoir. Jeannette is a precocious, ambitious, and resourceful child who does everything she can to survive and improve her family's situation. For most of her childhood, she is her father's favorite child because she encourages and believes in him. As the memoir progresses, she realizes that Dad and Mom do not have her best interests at heart, and she uses the independence her parents taught her to forge a life of her own.

Dad (Rex Walls)   Jeannette's charismatic but reckless father. Dad loves to speak of his own accomplishments, portraying himself as special and above the rules. However, he also refuses to keep a steady job and physically abuses Mom. As the memoir progresses, his alcoholism and irresponsibility put his family in the way of starvation and physical danger with increasing frequency. We later learn he had a difficult childhood and is very likely a survivor of sexual abuse.

Mom (Rose Mary Walls)   Jeannette's mother, a passionate artist and self-proclaimed "excitement addict." She is ambivalent about domestic responsibilities, such as cooking, cleaning, and disciplining children. She often tells the children to extend compassion to those who hurt them, but her definition of compassion involves never setting boundaries.

Lori Walls   Jeannette's sensible older sister, who questions Mom and Dad's parenting from an early age. Lori is intelligent and known for her quick, sarcastic remarks. She inherited Mom's passion for art, though she aspires to leave her family and live a more conventional lifestyle. She is the first Walls child to leave the family and go to New York City.

Brian Walls   Jeannette's little brother and constant companion. Brian likes to explore his surroundings and work outside. He and Jeannette regularly band together to survive by foraging for food, finding dry firewood, and occasionally stealing from neighbors. He follows Jeannette and Lori to New York City when he is a junior in high school.

Maureen Walls   Jeannette's beautiful youngest sibling. Unlike the other Walls siblings who bond together in the face of adversity, Maureen survives in Welch mostly by making friends and living with their families. Later in life, Maureen drops out of community college and tries to stab her mother. She spends a year in a mental institution and then moves to California.

Grandma Smith   Jeannette's maternal grandmother who often takes in the Walls family when they are down on their luck. Mom hated how strict and controlling she was as a mother, but Jeannette appreciates the structure whenever they visit.

Erma Walls   Jeannette's paternal grandmother, whom the family lives with when they first move to Welch. Erma is an angry, racist woman who has had a hard life and lashes out at the Walls children because of it. She sexually abuses Brian and may have inflicted similar abuse on her own children.

Dinitia Hewitt   A girl who attends Jeannette's school, and one of her few friends in Welch. Dinitia bullies Jeannette when the Walls family first moves to Welch, but the girls become friends after Jeannette defends one of Dinitia's neighbors from a dog. Because Dinitia is black, their friendship is unconventional in Welch, which is still very segregated.

Uncle Stanley   Dad's brother. He is kind to the Walls children when they live with Erma but then later molests Jeannette when she visits his house.

Billy Deel The Wallses' neighbor in Battle Mountain, a violent and aggressive boy who develops an infatuation with Jeannette. At only eleven years old, he already has a record as a juvenile delinquent. He actively pursues Jeannette romantically and tries to force himself on her when they play hide and seek. When Jeannette rejects him, he shoots at her and her siblings with his BB gun.

Grandpa Walls Dad's father, who worked on the railroad when Dad was a child. Unlike his wife, Erma, and his son, Stanley, Grandpa doesn't make much of an impression on Jeannette, neither abetting his wife's abuse nor challenging it.

Eric Jeannette's first husband, a kind, wealthy man who is practical and organized, in many ways the antithesis of Dad. Jeannette leaves Eric a year after her father dies.

John Jeannette's second husband, who admires her strength and scars. Like Jeannette, he is a writer.

Analysis of Major Characters

Jeannette Walls

Jeannette ties the story of her coming of age to her complicated feelings for her parents, showing her growth through their evolving relationship. More so than her siblings, Jeannette worships her parents and believes that they have her best interests at heart. As she begins to lose faith in them, Jeannette spares their feelings by picking up the slack herself, getting a job and managing finances without actively challenging their authority. She doesn't truly give up on them until her Dad whips her for actively calling Mom and Dad out on their negligence. From here on, she stops trying to save her family unit and works to save herself and her siblings. During her college years in New York, her hero worship of her parents transforms into anger and shame, both toward them and herself. She enacts this shame by marrying Eric, a wealthy man who shares almost nothing in common with her father. By Part V, Jeannette's anger has subsided into acceptance. Her choice to marry John, who admires her scars, demonstrates that she can now appreciate the difficulties she went through.

Throughout the memoir, Jeannette avoids drawing any straightforward conclusions about her childhood, reflecting the complicated way her parents both hurt and helped her. The undue suffering caused by her parents' recklessness produced the very qualities Jeannette needed to move to New York City and create a thriving journalism career out of nothing. Her happiness at the end, along with her continued relationship with her mother, shows that she considers her past to be like her scars: reflective of real pain but now only a sign that she survived. Jeannette's matter-of-fact narrative style also shows an inability to completely judge her parents. She recounts events as they happen, trying to capture how she felt about them at the time with very few moments of adult self-reflection. By not interjecting her adult perspective, she allows her childhood to speak for itself, neither actively condemning nor defending her parents. She instead leaves judgment up to the reader, suggesting that she cannot bring herself to do so.

Dad (Rex Walls)

Throughout the memoir, Dad reveals himself to be both a creative eccentric and a manipulative abuser. Dad has such a vivid presence in part because of the heroic persona he cultivates. Dad makes himself the center of every bedtime story, presenting himself as a storybook hero to his children instead of allowing them to admire fictional characters. His anger at Mom's disruption of these stories, then, reveals his deep reliance on his children's worship. Unfortunately, his desire for admiration also manifests as a need for control, leading to the physical and emotional abuse he inflicts on Mom, particularly when he drinks. As Dad's alcoholism worsens, the Walls family loses not only his income but also his optimism. Throughout Jeannette's childhood, Dad created hope for the family by promising to build them the titular Glass Castle. By their first winter in Welch, Dad allows the foundation his children dig for the castle to fill with garbage, showing an unwillingness to work toward a better life for his family.

While Dad appears to love Jeannette, he lacks the emotional tools to provide for her or support her as a parent. We can attribute some of Dad's shortcomings to the abuse he suffered as a child in Welch. Jeannette deduces that Erma likely molested Dad as a child, leading to his anger at Brian for suffering the same fate. Erma's uninterest in her grandchildren and anger toward the world suggest that Dad may have had a loveless childhood as the unjust target of Erma's rage. This revelation could explain his adulthood need for admiration and refusal to take responsibility, since Dad grew up with no role models for how to be a loving parent or how to show love in a healthy way. Toward the end of his life, Dad attempts reconciliation with Jeannette. He contributes to her college tuition, saving her from dropping out of school and providing for her like a parent. He also shows interest in her journalism career and tries to help with stories, partially recreating their bond. He never reaches hero-level status again in Jeannette's eyes, but Jeannette decides before he dies that he loved her in his own way.

Mom (Rose Mary Walls)

Mom has a deeply philosophical nature, analyzing the meaning behind the actions she takes. However, as her selfishness becomes evident throughout Jeannette's childhood, we realize that she uses philosophy primarily as a tool to absolve herself from both blame and responsibility. This paradigm is most evident in her constant insistence on compassion. At first, Mom's belief that the children must show compassion to people who actively hurt them, like Billy Deel or Erma, seems kind but dangerous. However, when Jeannette realizes that Mom simply doesn't want to upset Erma and have to search for a new home, we realize that Mom's call for compassion helps her avoid confrontation and conflict. In this way, she uses her beliefs as a justification for choosing her own comfort and safety over her children's. Mom is a victim of Dad's physical and emotional abuse, a fact that she also attempts to hide with philosophy. Mom explains her choice to stay with Dad as being an "excitement addict," intentionally using the word addiction to evoke Dad's alcoholism. As the family has given up trying to get Dad sober, Mom's phrasing here implies that she can do nothing to change or leave her relationship with Dad.

CHARACTER ANALYSIS

Themes, Motifs & Symbols

Themes

Themes are the fundamental and often universal ideas explored in a literary work.

Strength from Hardship

Throughout the memoir, Mom and Dad claim that their hands-off parenting style will contribute to the ultimate betterment of their children because danger and hardship build character and resilience. While nothing can justify their parents' neglect, the children's hard fight for survival helps them later in life, making it difficult to entirely dismiss Mom and Dad's assertion. We see this philosophy play out when Dad throws Jeannette in the Hot Pot over and over until she figures out how to swim. While Jeannette reacts with fear and anger immediately after this swimming lesson, Dad points out that she did, in fact, learn how to swim, implying that a positive result justifies the short-term trauma. Ultimately, the suffering caused by their parents' recklessness produces the very qualities Jeannette and Lori need to move to New York City and create thriving careers out of nothing. For example, Jeannette's experiences fighting bullies on the streets of Welch prepare her to face muggers in the South Bronx. John's admiration of Jeannette's scar also evokes this philosophy because he believes that this physical proof of suffering signifies her strength. In this way, the hardship Jeannette went through also helps her find love and acceptance.

Compassion versus Boundaries

According to Mom's philosophy, extending compassion to a person who has been through trauma requires allowing them to take their anger out on you without consequence As it relates to her marriage, Mom's way of showing compassionate acceptance of Dad's alcoholism means accepting the life of poverty, instability, physical danger, and starvation he inflicts on the family. Mom encourages similar behavior when she reminds Jeannette that Billy Deel comes from a broken home and deserves kindness. Accordingly, Jeannette tries to show compassion by accepting Billy's affection, which leads to him shooting a BB gun at her and her siblings. Jeannette begins to reject this conditioning when she refuses to forgive Erma for her racist opinions and abuse. When Uncle Stanley molests Jeannette, she doesn't take Mom's advice to allow his attacks simply because he's lonely, but prioritizes her safety and avoids him. By the end of the memoir, Jeannette has learned to extend empathy without putting herself in danger, as evidenced by her continued relationship with her parents. While she continues to see them, she doesn't allow them to live with her, both accepting them for who they are and protecting herself.

ABUSE

Jeannette explores the way abusive relationships create a self-perpetuating cycle of abuse across generations. For example, Mom points out that many of the frightening people they meet, such as Billy Deel, come from broken households and abusive situations, meaning that their bad home lives contributed to their violent characters. Dad's family in particular demonstrates the way abuse gets passed on through generations. Erma drinks constantly, suggesting that alcoholism runs in the family. When Dad takes Erma's side after she molests Brian, the children deduce that Erma likely sexually abused Dad. Uncle Stanley also demonstrates sexually predatory behavior, implying that he also may have been a victim. However, Mom reveals that the chain of abuse did not begin with Erma. Orphaned as a young child, Erma lived with a string of aunts and uncles who mistreated her for the rest of her childhood, and she took her pent-up rage out on her own children. This tragic pattern of abusers begetting abusers demonstrates the cyclical nature of abuse. When Jeannette and Lori protect Brian from Erma and refuse to ignore what happened, they offer us hope that the cycle can be broken.

MOTIFS

> *Motifs are recurring structures, contrasts, or literary devices that can help to develop and inform the text's major themes.*

FIRE

Dangerous fires appear throughout Jeannette's childhood, highlighting the danger Mom and Dad's negligence places their children in. At three years old, Jeannette catches on fire while cooking unsupervised, and after the incident she becomes obsessed with starting small fires. Mom and Dad encourage Jeannette's fascination with fire and claim it shows bravery in the face of adversity. This rhetoric hides their culpability for Jeannette's accident by implying that fire attacked Jeannette, instead of acknowledging that a three-year-old shouldn't use a stove. The family's hotel in San Francisco catches fire when Jeannette is four, and she starts to worry that all fire has a grudge against her. Here, she assigns agency to fire, imitating her parents by blaming fire for attacking her. When Jeannette and Brian set a batch of hazardous waste on fire and almost burn to death, Dad finally acknowledges fire as a natural force by explaining what happened in terms of physics. His assertion that "no rules apply" at the chaos they've created with their fire means that the usual Walls philosophy of showing no fear cannot apply to an explosion.

ANIMALS

The Walls family adopts dozens of animals over the course of the memoir, and the animals' ill-fated ends display the family's unhealthy living situations. When flies infest their house in Battle Mountain, Jeannette asks about getting a No-Pest Strip to kill them. Mom refuses on the grounds that what kills the flies likely will hurt humans too. Mom's policy against animal repellents in the house may appear logical, but it ignores the toxic conditions the humans in the family face. Most of the family's animals, including their dog Juju, can't survive in Blythe, where the Wallses live for several months. Dad drowns a litter of kittens the family cannot afford to take care of, displaying a cruel disregard for their lives when they become inconvenient. In Welch, the house gets so cold that Brian's iguana freezes to death. The Wallses routinely live in environments that kill animals, both passively and actively, which means, by Mom's judgment, they can't be very good for the Walls family either.

HYPOCRISY

As Jeannette grows throughout the memoir and notices the repeated instances of hypocrisy in her parents' behavior, she realizes convenience and desperation create hypocrites. More often than not, Mom and Dad change their values to serve their immediate needs. Jeannette explicitly makes this connection when Mom says they have to tolerate Erma's racist rants because they would be homeless without her. In another instance of this, Mom believes that Lori's poor eyesight means she should exercise her eyes instead of buying glasses, but changes her mind as soon as the school offers to pay for Lori's glasses. Mom finds the prospect of getting something for free

MOTIFS

tempting enough to change her opinion. Furthermore, when Jeannette and Lori attack Erma after she molests Brian, Dad admonishes them for disrespecting their grandmother. Dad's unhinged response contradicts the lessons he teaches his children about "Pervert Hunting" and never showing the enemy fear. In this instance, Dad's hypocrisy likely stems from his deeply repressed sexual trauma, demonstrating that his emotional need to diminish and ignore what happened to him takes precedence over protecting Brian.

SYMBOLS

Symbols are objects, characters, figures, or colors used to represent abstract ideas or concepts.

THE GLASS CASTLE

For much of Jeannette's childhood, Dad's promise to build the Glass Castle represents both the family's hope and Jeannette's hero worship of Dad, but, as Jeannette grows older, the castle comes to symbolize his broken promises. Like Dad's bedtime stories that portray him as a hero, the image of a glass castle seems larger than life and carries fairy-tale connotations. Jeannette cannot help but believe in Dad's beautiful plan because as a child she sees Dad as the man from his stories, brilliant and talented. Jeannette's belief in the Glass Castle and her faith in her father both disappear around the time that the family starts dumping garbage in the hole meant for the foundation. The construction of a glass castle requires not just imaginative genius, but also the dedication and effort Dad lacks. As time passes and Dad's alcoholism reaches crushing new lows, the Glass Castle turns into a symbol of impossible dreams, fragile as glass.

STARS

Dad giving the children stars as Christmas gifts represents both the family's anti-materialistic values and their belief in their own specialness. Mom and Dad insist the stars make better gifts than toys because the stars will last forever. While Dad likely decided on the star ruse to make up for his inability to afford gifts, it is consistent with the Walls family's philosophy that prioritizes experience and adventure over material possessions. Accordingly, we see the true value of the gift lies in the moment each child has with Dad in which he shares his knowledge of space. Nevertheless, Dad's claiming of the stars has a dark side of entitlement. He tells Jeannette that he can give the kids the stars because no one has claimed them yet, comparing the gift to Christopher Columbus claiming the Americas. However, Columbus didn't claim empty land; he stole land already occupied by multiple nations. Dad's star gifts are false as well because the stars cannot belong to the Walls children simply because Dad says so. In this sense, the stars represent Dad's belief that they are exceptional people whom the rules don't apply to.

THE JOSHUA TREE

The Joshua tree symbolizes Jeannette and the extreme environment she grows up in, as Joshua trees grow gnarled and almost entirely sideways in the desert's harsh winds. When Jeannette wants to dig up a sapling and replant it in a less extreme environment where it could grow straight and tall, her impulse suggests that she might also prefer a less hazardous upbringing. Mom's insistence that a protected Joshua tree would lose what makes it special reveals her larger philosophy that strength and beauty come from hardship. When Jeannette creates a more ideal environment for herself in New York City, she must reconcile her new surroundings with her identity as a person shaped by harsh conditions. In this light, we can read her rejection of Eric, with his stability and wealth, as an acceptance of at least some of Mom's ideas about the Joshua tree. Jeannette marries John, who sees her scars as proof of Jeannette's strength, which echoes her mother's view of the beauty of the Joshua tree.

SYMBOLS

Summary & Analysis

Part I: Woman on the Street & Part II: The Desert

Summary: Part I

Jeannette Walls begins her memoir with a scene from adulthood. While in a taxi in New York City on a cold evening in March, she wonders if she has overdressed for the party she will be attending. When she looks out the window, she sees her mother, dressed in rags and picking through a dumpster. Jeannette slides down in her seat to avoid being recognized and asks the driver to take her home.

Inside her upscale apartment, Jeannette is overwhelmed by guilt and self-loathing for living so comfortably while her parents are homeless. She calls Mom, and they meet for lunch at a Chinese restaurant to discuss if there's anything Jeannette can do to help. Mom refuses her offer, maintaining that she and Dad are living the way they want to. Mom urges Jeannette to accept her family as they are and to be honest about who she is.

Summary: Part II

In Part II, Jeannette goes back to her very first memory, which takes place when Jeannette is three years old and living in a trailer park in southern Arizona. While she boils hot dogs over the stove, the tutu she is wearing catches fire, engulfing her in flames. Her mother smothers the flames with a blanket, and the neighbor rushes them to the hospital. At the hospital, the doctors say Jeannette is lucky to be alive, and they perform a skin graft, replacing the skin on Jeannette's badly burned sides with skin from her thighs.

Mom, Dad, her older sister Lori, and her younger brother Brian visit when they can, and they usually cause a scene. They talk and argue in loud voices, and on one occasion Dad physically threatens one of the doctors because he doesn't think they should use so many bandages on Jeannette's burns. At the end of her six-week hospital stay, Dad rushes her out of the hospital without paying, a scheme he calls "checking out Rex Walls-style." At home, Jeannette goes right back to cooking hot dogs without supervision and develops a fascination with fire, playing with matches and setting and putting out small fires in the yard. A couple months later, Dad wakes up the whole family in the middle of the night and tells them they have to leave town. They sleep outside that night without pillows, and Dad says it will give them good posture like the Indians.

The Wallses often leave town in the middle of the night, which Dad calls "doing the skedaddle." Dad struggles to keep a job for very long, so they move every couple of months, usually to stay ahead of the bill collectors. Sometimes the family goes to Phoenix to stay with Jeannette's maternal grandmother, but Dad and Grandma Smith argue often, so they never stay long. They spend most of their time in various desert mining towns. In the desert, Mom and Dad teach the kids reading and mathematics as well as specialized survival skills, such as how to forage for food and shoot pistols. They don't wear shoes or use toothbrushes, and the family eats irregularly. Once, when a vineyard owner in California allows people to come and pick their own grapes for five cents a pound, the family eats nothing but green grapes for weeks.

ANALYSIS: PART I & PART II

The striking wealth disparity in the memoir's opening scene grabs the reader's attention by introducing the confusing relationship between Jeannette and her mother. Though dramatic in its juxtaposition, an encounter between a wealthy New Yorker in a cab and a homeless woman is nevertheless a familiar image because in major metropolitan cities extreme prosperity and poverty often exist in close proximity. However, Jeannette turns this image on its head when she casually refers to the dispossessed woman as "Mom," and then later walks into her own luxurious apartment building only a few blocks away. Because of their relationship, the extreme differences in their respective lives appear not only unjust but also cruel. Furthermore, Jeannette's memories of her mother painting in the desert, reading Shakespeare, and refusing financial assistance undermine a long list of stereotypes about people experiencing homelessness. By the time these two women bicker about cosmetic hair removal treatments in a Chinese restaurant, we may find their relationship puzzling and confusing. The strange nature of their encounter, then, causes the reader to wonder how this could happen, encouraging us to continue reading in order to discover the answer.

The opening of Part I sets the tone for the memoir in both content and style. This fire marks the first of many accidental fires in

Jeannette's childhood, emphasizing the constant danger that permeates her life. The incident both raises concerns about the lack of parental supervision Jeannette had and also causes us to marvel at her independence in cooking hot dogs at three, a pattern of fear and admiration that will become familiar by the end of the memoir. The first statement—"I was on fire"—establishes the innocent and detached tone of Jeannette's narration. Rather than project her adult thoughts and feelings onto events, Jeannette recounts her memories as objectively as possible. The blunt style mimics the way young children take their surroundings for granted because they lack the frame of reference to understand what is normal. In addition, the lack of commentary creates an underlying mood of dread. Without Jeannette's adult voice, we have no choice but to watch the events of her childhood with no intervention or analysis from a voice of reason. We begin to wonder if someone will intervene and when Jeannette will realize that she is in danger.

Jeannette's first memories also introduce each character's idiosyncrasies and subtle differences, laying the groundwork for the interpersonal conflict to come. Dad's tendency to recast hardships as benefits, as when he tells the kids that sleeping outside without pillows will help them have good posture, suggests an inability to acknowledge flaws and mistakes. Jeannette's desire to continue their nomadic lifestyle forever demonstrates that she believes Dad's explanations and introduces her hero worship of her father. When Lori responds that she thinks they may truly live in a nomadic way forever, the reader can pick up on an underlying current of pessimism, hinting at a rift between Dad and Lori. Mom works to smooth over tensions by excusing Dad's unceremonious abandonment of the family cat and distracting the children with songs, showing a tendency to minimize and distract from Dad's harm. Brian's silence and fear for the family dog hints that although he is younger than Jeannette, Brian already has lost some faith in Dad. By the end of this section, we have a complex portrait of a family that lives very precariously and whose members appear to be operating on conflicting levels of awareness of that fact.

Part II: The Desert, continued (Explanation of Glass Castle to San Francisco)

Summary

I wondered if the fire were out to get me. I wondered
if all fire was related, like Dad said all humans were
related ... I didn't have the answers to those questions,
but what I did know was that I lived in a world that at
any moment could erupt into fire.

(See QUOTATIONS, *p. 49)*

Dad promises that the family's nomadic, adventurous life is temporary and that one day they will strike it rich by using the Prospector,
a gold-hunting contraption he plans to invent. On occasion, Dad
spends what little money they have on liquor, drinks too much, and
comes home in a violent rage. Despite his periodic bad behavior, the
kids admire him and love to listen to him tell stories about his past
heroics. His sworn objective is to build his family the Glass Castle,
a large home made of glass, complete with solar panels and a water-
purification system.

Dad grew up in Welch, an old coal mining town in West Virginia,
and left when he turned seventeen to join the air force and become a
pilot. He met Mom when he saw her dive off a canyon to a lake forty
feet below and jumped in after her. They got married six months
later. Jeannette finds this romantic, but Mom says that Dad wouldn't
take no for an answer, and she was just trying to get away from her
mother. She also frequently notes that Dad pawned her wedding
ring. Dad promises to buy her a new one when he finds gold.

After they got married, Dad left the air force because he wanted
to make more money. Mom quickly had four children, each one
year apart: Lori, Mary Charlene, Jeannette, and Brian. Mary
Charlene died of crib death when she was an infant, and Mom says
Jeannette was born to replace her. Mom speaks cavalierly about
Mary Charlene's death, but Dad never recovered. After her death,
he started drinking frequently and lost every job he got.

When Jeannette is four years old, Dad decides they should move
to Las Vegas so he can make some money for the Prospector in the
casinos. On the way to Vegas, Mom and Dad stop at a bar in Nevada

and leave the kids in the car. When they return and continue on the road, Dad drives over some railroad tracks, and Jeannette goes flying out of the back seat. She sits on the roadside bleeding, sore, and afraid for an indeterminate amount of time before Dad realizes she's gone and returns to retrieve her. He refers to her bloody nose as a "snot locker," and the whole family laughs.

In Vegas, the family lives in a hotel for about a month. Dad makes a lot of money, and says he has a system for winning at the blackjack tables. Every day, Dad buys the kids presents and takes them out to eat. Eventually, one of the dealers figures out Dad's scheme, and they have to do the skedaddle (Dad's term for leaving in the middle of the night).

Dad says that the Mafia will be after them, so they go all the way to San Francisco next. They stay in another hotel, where the kids play all day while Mom and Dad are out. In the hotel, Jeannette plays with matches and sets small fires in the toilet. One night, she wakes up and discovers the curtain over her head has caught fire. Dad saves everyone and helps put out the fire. Jeannette worries that fire may be targeting her personally, noticing that her life is especially chaotic.

ANALYSIS

This section introduces Dad's dream of building the Glass Castle, which represents a hope of future stability and happiness for the family. Even at this early stage, several red flags suggest that Dad will never actually build the Glass Castle. For example, he plans to fund its construction with a gold-finding Prospector device that he always seems to be working on. Because Dad never appears to make any progress on the device, we start to wonder whether he has a concrete idea of how to create it at all. In addition, Dad's plan to strike gold in the desert in the 1960s reads as anachronistic and romantic, more like a story of the Wild West than the mid-twentieth century. Dad's promise to buy Mom a new wedding ring when he finds gold also casts doubt on his Glass Castle plans. Dad uses the offer of a new ring to shut down Mom's anger over his pawning of her wedding ring, which makes it sound like an excuse instead of an actual pledge. If we do not believe Dad's intent to buy a new ring for Mom, we must also wonder if he truly believes he will build the Glass Castle.

Mom's brief interjections to Dad's bedtime stories raise questions about the stability of their marriage. Dad's anger at Mom when she rolls her eyes at the stories makes him seem both insecure and dangerous. Mom's sarcasm draws attention to her need to undermine him. She has not yet intervened in any of Dad's upsetting antics, such as abandoning the cat, but instead attacks his self-important bedtime stories, an act which ultimately only hurts his ego. Her passive-aggressive approach indicates an unhealthy dynamic where she provokes Dad but doesn't actually challenge him. Furthermore, their conflicting interpretations of his marriage proposal suggest that he harassed and bullied Mom into marrying him. Therefore, when Mom says she didn't know life with Dad would be worse than life with her own overbearing mother, we understand that she traded one overbearing and controlling person in her life for another. Mom and Dad clearly have unhealthy and abusive patterns in the way they relate to each other, which adds a sense of foreboding to what is to come.

When the San Francisco hotel catches fire, Jeannette's fascination with fire turns into a fear that the element itself wants to hurt her. This personification of fire indicates that Jeannette has identified her life as uniquely chaotic but cannot yet understand the true source of this chaos. Her confusion may partially come from the way her parents encourage her to play with fire after her hospital stay in order to conquer her fear, displacing the blame of what hurt Jeannette onto the fire and not the lack of supervision. Dad even describes her hospital stay at age three as her having won a fight with fire, as if fire were an opponent that actively attacked Jeannette. Interestingly, Jeannette wonders about a kinship between the fires, recognizing instinctively that they have a common source. However, the true common denominator between the fires is her parents' negligence. Jeannette's observation that her life could catch fire at any moment also indicates that she has noticed the instability in her life, but just as before, she cannot identify that Mom and Dad, not fire, create the unpredictability.

PART II: THE DESERT, CONTINUED (SAN FRANCISCO TO BLYTHE)

SUMMARY

After the fire in San Francisco, the Walls family spends a couple of nights sleeping in their car on the beach, and then drives toward the Mojave Desert. On the way, Mom makes them stop the car because a Joshua tree catches her eye. It is a gnarled tree, grown sideways because of the environment's harsh winds. Mom thinks it's so beautiful that she has to paint it immediately. Jeannette tells Mom that she wants to get a Joshua tree sapling and protect it so that it will grow upright. Mom admonishes her that to do so would ruin the tree's beauty. Dad drives a little up the road from the tree and finds a place for them to live, there in Midland.

At night the sounds of coyotes keep Jeannette awake. One night, she thinks she hears something slithering under her bed. When she runs out to tell her father, he tells Jeannette that it's the same Demon that has been chasing him for years, and they run outside to chase the Demon with his hunting knife. Dad says all Jeannette has to do is show the Demon that she's not afraid.

Dad gets a job in a gypsum mine and comes home covered in white dust. At home, he plays "ghost" with the kids and gives Mom sacks of gypsum for her sculptures. Mom gets pregnant and spends her days working on her art. She writes stories and plays, and Lori helps her proofread them.

Dad loses his job at the gypsum mine, and when Christmas comes, they have no money. For their Christmas presents, Dad takes each kid outside individually and lets them pick out their favorite star in the sky. That night, Dad teaches the kids all about light-years, black holes, and the special qualities of each of their stars.

On the way to Blythe, Mom and Dad get into an argument because Mom says she has been pregnant for ten months. When Dad swears at and ridicules her, Mom bolts out of the car, and Dad chases her through the desert brush in the car with the kids in the back seat. He eventually corners her against a boulder with his car and drags Mom back inside, sobbing.

Mom and Dad make up the next day and move into a cinder block apartment building in Blythe. Most of the families are Spanish-speaking migrant farm workers. The kids enroll in school, and one day a group of Mexican girls jump Jeannette for being a skinny teacher's pet. The next day, Brian beats the girls off with a yucca branch, and Jeannette cracks a girl's skull with a big rock.

Mom gives birth to a girl, Maureen. A few months later, Dad announces they're moving to Battle Mountain to find gold. They rent a giant U-Haul truck for the journey, and all four children ride in the back with the furniture. The back is cold and dark, and Maureen cries the whole way. Several hours into the journey, the back doors fly open, and the children have to hold onto the Prospector so they don't get sucked out. Eventually, a car pulls up beside the trailer and the driver flags down Mom and Dad. Dad yells at the kids for not being more careful, relocks the back, and continues driving.

ANALYSIS

Mom and Jeannette's diverging opinions about the Joshua tree reveal a difference in their respective life philosophies. Joshua trees, like the one Mom stops to paint, grow gnarled and almost entirely sideways due to the desert's harsh winds. When Jeannette wants to dig up a sapling and replant it in a less extreme environment, one in which it could grow "nice and tall and straight," her impulse suggests that she might also prefer a less hazardous upbringing. This isn't the first time Jeannette has shown a proclivity for neatness and order. Whereas Mom hates Grandma Smith's strict rules, Jeannette appreciates the structure. And whereas Dad distrusts hospitals, Jeannette likes how clean and orderly they are. Mom's belief that the Joshua tree's struggle creates its beauty reflects her commitment to a life of upheaval. It also indicates that Mom will never offer Jeannette the kind of protection she might like to have because Mom admires strength gained through adversity.

Dad's stories and antics throughout Part II portray him as both a creative eccentric and a manipulative abuser. His gift of stars to the children at Christmas epitomizes this tension. On the one hand, Dad offers each child a bonding moment with him where he shares his knowledge of space and makes them feel special, a beautiful way of salvaging a Christmas without money for material gifts. However, he cannot truly give his children the stars. In addition, he encourages his children to look down on those who get material gifts, trying to disguise the reality of the family's poverty and his shortcomings by pretending superiority. While the star gifts actually do end up being a lovely memory, the episode demonstrates Dad's habit of pretending his difficulties and shortcomings are actually intentional or even signs of genius. This pattern echoes the way he portrays the fact that he relentlessly pursued Mom into marriage as a romantic gesture and tries to distract Jeannette from her trauma of falling out of the car with a joke about her nose. In both those instances, as with the star gifts, Dad covers up frightening realities with his charm.

The two car rides in this section further characterize Mom and Dad as extremely selfish and reckless. When Mom jumps out of the car while it's still moving, she demonstrates disregard for her own safety and her children's safety over a petty argument about gestation times. Her willingness to leave the other children with Dad in his angry state also suggests she prioritizes her own anger and whims over her children. Dad's decision to pursue her with the car not only demonstrates drunken, abusive recklessness, but a dangerous desire to maintain control of his wife at all costs. In this event, Dad and Mom both demonstrate that they care more about perpetuating their dynamic and continuing their arguments than protecting and considering the safety and feelings of their children. When Mom and Dad illegally put all four children, including a newborn infant, in the back of a U-Haul with no seatbelts, food, or water for several hours, they reach a new level of child endangerment. Their commitment to such a dangerous plan demonstrates more concern for their own comfort and thrift than their children. This scene thus casts a foreboding shadow over what is to come in Battle Mountain.

PART II: THE DESERT, CONTINUED (BATTLE MOUNTAIN)

SUMMARY

Maybe I should have cut him some slack. With his broken wing and a lifetime of eating roadkill, he probably had a lot to be ungrateful about. Too much hard luck can create a permanent meanness of spirit in any creature.

(See QUOTATIONS, p. 49)

In Battle Mountain, Dad gets a decent job in the barite mine. The owner of the barite mine also owns the Wallses' house and the commissary, so he deducts rent and food out of Dad's weekly paycheck. Mom only cooks occasionally, usually one large pot of beans meant to last all week. Dad drinks less and stays home with the family in the evenings. Strays and wild animals such as lizards, coyotes, and buzzards come in and out of the house.

One afternoon, while exploring the nearby dump, Brian and Jeannette mix together various hazardous waste liquids in an old shed and set it on fire. The flame quickly grows out of control, and Brian gets stuck in the shed while Jeannette runs for help. She finds Dad, who kicks in a wall and rescues Brian.

A few weeks later, Dad takes the family to a natural sulfur spring called the Hot Pot and teaches Jeannette how to swim by throwing her into the spring and letting her sink again and again. The process terrifies and infuriates Jeannette, and at first she refuses to allow him to hug her. When Dad insists he loves her and only wanted to teach her independence, she quickly forgives him.

Jeannette and Brian become fascinated by the Green Lantern, the local brothel. They do not yet know about sex, but Mom tells them that the women who work there do bad things, piquing their interest. They attempt to spy on the Green Lantern, but learn nothing about what goes on inside.

After six months in Battle Mountain, Dad loses his job. He disappears for long stretches of time, saying he is looking for gold. The family starts to go hungry, and the kids resort to stealing food from classmates and neighbors. When Mom finally confronts Dad about not providing for his family, they have a long and violent screaming match that lasts through the night. In the end, they decide that Mom will start teaching.

Mom makes good money teaching, but Dad often confiscates Mom's paychecks and spends them on elaborate family dinners and alcohol. For Brian's birthday, Dad buys him a comic book and takes him to dinner with Ginger, a woman who works at the Green Lantern. Later, Dad disappears with Ginger in a hotel bedroom. When Brian tells Jeannette about his birthday dinner, he says that Ginger is stupid, but refuses to elaborate what about his encounter with Ginger upset him.

A boy named Billy Deel moves to Battle Mountain. He is known to be a juvenile delinquent and develops a crush on Jeannette. One day, he invites Jeannette into his house to look at his father, who has passed out on a mattress with his genitals hanging out and his jeans soaked with urine. When she tells her mother about the incident, Mom tells her to show Billy more compassion. Later, Billy gives Jeannette a ring made out of real silver and turquoise. One day, while Jeannette plays hide and seek with the neighbors, Billy forces his way into Jeannette's cramped hiding spot, kisses her, and tries to undress her. She fights him off and goes to his house the next day to return the ring.

The next day, Billy comes to the house with a BB gun and starts shooting at the house. To retaliate, Lori grabs Dad's pistol and shoots it at Billy's feet. As he runs away, Jeannette grabs the pistol and shoots at him too. The neighbors call in the incident, and the police come by with Mom and Dad to tell them they need to come by the magistrate the next morning. That night, they pack up and leave for Phoenix.

> *Dad told us that zone was known in physics as the*
> *boundary between turbulence and order. "It's the*
> *place where no rules apply, or at least they haven't*
> *figured 'em out yet," he said. "You-all got a little too*
> *close to it today."*
>
> *(See QUOTATIONS, p. 50)*

ANALYSIS

Dad's job at the barite mine reveals a societal layer to the Walls family's poverty because of the mine's exploitative treatment of its workers. In Battle Mountain, as Jeannette explains it, the Wallses live in a mining camp, where the company owns the miners' homes and the commissary, the only place to buy groceries. Because the mine determines their employees' wages and cost of living, the mine can adjust prices to drive miners into debt, essentially making them indentured servants. Dad rarely drinks when they first move to Battle Mountain, and yet they consistently run out of money and some-times owe the mine on payday. Between the commissary's prices and Mom and Dad's terrible budgeting skills, the family has no real opportunity to profit from Dad's job. While Mom and Dad often unfairly scapegoat the government and society for creating their problems, the mining camp's financial system shows that structural issues worsen the Walls family's situation.

Dad's assessment of Jeannette and Brian's fire as them getting too close to "the boundary between turbulence and order" provides a use-ful description of the Walls children's lives. Dad speaks to Jeannette and Brian in a quiet and grave tone, which may indicate that he was afraid for their lives, or it could also suggest a moment of self-reflection. Dad intentionally subjects his kids to a life of chaos and lawlessness, not unlike the boundary between turbulence and order, and this inci-dent left Brian closer to death than his usual antics. Unlike with the fire in Jeannette's first memory, Dad characterizes this explosion as an elemental force instead of an adversary. His recognition that the explo-sion is not something the children can fight but something they should avoid comes close to admitting that sometimes staying in the realm of rules and order is necessary for safety. Unfortunately, he never fol-lows through on this realization, and maintains the family's status quo.

Around this part of the memoir, Jeannette begins to question Dad's infallibility, particularly at the Hot Pot. At first when Dad throws Jeannette into the water, she reaches for him, instinctively counting on her father to keep her safe. Her surprise and fear at Dad's repeated throwing shows that while Dad intended to teach Jeannette to swim, he actually taught Jeannette that he was willing to hurt her. After Jeannette's terrifying ordeal, she doesn't immediately allow Dad to hug her, a great contrast to her instant glee at Dad's "snot locker" comment when she falls out of the car. Her hesitation to forgive Dad marks the first moment she questions his heroism and his ability to protect her. When Dad asks Jeannette why he would throw her into the water if not for her betterment, he equates her frustration over a traumatic experience with doubting his love, effectively manipulating Jeannette into forgiving him. Here Jeannette begins to learn that some of the fear and suffering Dad creates is because of his personal failures, and not for any greater purpose.

At this point, no one has talked to Jeannette about sex, and yet her unstructured upbringing has brought sexuality to her attention in ways that are both confusing and traumatizing. Mom's explanation that "bad things" happen at the Green Lantern both intrigues and frightens Jeannette and Brian, leading them to spy on the women. Although Jeannette doesn't understand what the women do, this early depiction of sex portrays it as something hurtful. Brian's later anger at Ginger only increases Jeannette's confusion because he refuses to explain why he's angry. Although discussing the Green Lantern had once been a shared experience, Brian's newfound understanding of sex work divides Jeannette and Brian. In this way, Jeannette's early encounters with sex involve discomfort and isolation. Jeannette's other early introduction to sexuality comes from Billy Deel. At only eleven, Billy acts sexually precocious, likely because of negative influence from his alcoholic father. When he forcibly kisses Jeannette, he calls it "rape," increasing Jeannette's association of sex with violence.

PART II: THE DESERT, CONTINUED (PHOENIX)

SUMMARY

I could hear people around us whispering about the crazy drunk man and his dirty little urchin children, but who cared what they thought? None of them had ever had their hand licked by a cheetah.

(See QUOTATIONS, p. 50)

SUMMARY & ANALYSIS

As the Wallses drive to Phoenix, Jeannette looks forward to staying with Grandma Smith. Jeannette appreciates the structure and regular meals her grandmother provides. On the way, however, Mom reveals that Grandma Smith died months previously, and they are going to live in a property she inherited from the estate. Mom doesn't understand why Jeannette is upset.

Mom inherited a 14-bedroom adobe property and a large sum of money, which she mostly spends on art supplies. Dad gets a steady job and joins an electricians' union. He buys the children bicycles. The school buys Lori glasses, and she becomes obsessed with drawing all the details she is finally able to see. In school, the administration places the children in gifted classes.

Despite their material comfort, the Wallses' house is infested with termites. The house also lacks air conditioning, so they leave the doors and windows open at night. One night, a neighbor walks up to Jeannette's room and molests her. Dad runs outside with Brian and Jeannette to chase down the offender, an activity they call Pervert Hunting. However, Mom and Dad still insist on keeping the doors and windows open at night.

After about a year in Phoenix, Dad starts drinking more and causing scenes in public. He shouts during Mass, and, once, breaks into the cheetah's cage at the Phoenix Zoo. He loses his job around this time, and money is tight, but when Christmas comes, Mom and the kids are able to buy a tree and small presents for everyone. On Christmas Day, Dad drinks so much that he shouts blasphemous curses during Christmas Mass, and when they get home, he lights the Christmas tree on fire, destroying all the presents.

For her tenth birthday, Jeannette asks Dad to stop drinking as her birthday present. Dad ties himself to his bed to detox and is sober and healthy after a couple weeks. Though Brian and Lori are skeptical of their father's commitment to sobriety, Jeannette believes that he will stay sober because it was his birthday present to her.

The family plans an exciting extended trip to the Grand Canyon, but the car breaks down on the way, and they are forced to walk home. An older woman picks them up and gives them a ride home, more than once referring to them as poor people. Jeannette retorts that they are not poor. Dad disappears as soon as they get home, and returns blackout drunk the next morning, dragging Mom from her hiding spot and tackling her to the ground. The kids hit Dad and try to make him stop, but he pins Mom down and makes her admit that she loves him. She eventually succumbs and the two embrace.

Mom receives a check from the oil company that leases some property she inherited from Grandma Smith, and she buys a car for $200. She plans to move the family to West Virginia, where she hopes Dad's family will be able to help them. Dad opposes the idea at first, but ultimately agrees to go with them.

Analysis

Jeannette's time in Phoenix increases her doubts about her parents. Before the Walls family moved to Phoenix, Dad swore that the only thing preventing him from building the Glass Castle was a lack of capital, yet when Mom's grand inheritance arrives and Dad gets a good union job, all discussion of the Prospector and the Glass Castle disappears. Dad's lack of follow-through on his beautiful dream demonstrates a streak of laziness or perhaps implies that he never truly intended to build the castle at all. Furthermore, Mom and Dad's unwillingness to work leads them to allow the house to fall into disarray, allowing termites to fester until they become a danger. The family's inability to maintain stability even when given financial resources demonstrates that Mom and Dad are ultimately incapable of long-term planning and investment. When Jeannette asks Dad to quit drinking as her tenth birthday present, she discovers that not even love is proof against disappointment. To his credit, Dad makes an earnest attempt to quit, emphasizing that he does truly love Jeannette. Unfortunately, alcoholism makes no concessions for love, making this another lesson in her parents' fallibility.

The Pervert Hunting incident demonstrates how Mom and Dad actively teach their children to avoid setting boundaries that could keep them safe. Jeannette explicitly compares the activity to her childhood Demon Hunting adventures with Dad in Blythe. Dad used Demon Hunting to teach Jeannette that the best way to deal with an enemy was to show it no fear, an aggressive, reactive approach to handling adversity. Whereas facing an imaginary demon with pluck and anger may teach courage, chasing down real intruders could put Jeannette in greater danger. Even though the neighborhood prowlers are a very real threat to Jeannette's safety, Mom and Dad refuse to close the doors and windows at night or to provide any practical solutions beyond vigilante "hunting." Their belief that locking the door would mean giving in to fear creates a definition of courage that equates protecting oneself as cowardly. This paradigm echoes their reaction to Jeannette setting herself on fire: better to be brave and put oneself in danger than to be a safe coward.

Jeannette's reaction to Dad breaking into the cheetah cage shows why it is difficult for her to let go of her hero worship of him. Because Dad portrays himself as having exceptional intelligence that makes him above the rules, Jeannette believes that following Dad's teachings makes her exceptional too. She demonstrates how seductive she finds this view of the world in her reaction to the spectators at the zoo. When Jeannette notices the onlookers gossiping about her father's drunkenness and her dirty appearance, she makes no note of any fear they might have had for the Walls children's safety. Since we can assume that at least some of the spectators worried about children in a cheetah cage, Jeannette's omission of these comments seems deliberate. By focusing only on the cosmetic comments, Jeannette can easily dismiss the onlookers in much the same way that she dismissed children who didn't get stars for Christmas. Just as the children who got material gifts missed out on getting stars, these onlookers with their shallow conformity don't get the exciting experience of a cheetah licking them.

PART III: WELCH (ERMA'S HOUSE)

SUMMARY

> *"You should never hate anyone, even your worst*
> *enemies. Everyone has something good about them.*
> *You have to find the redeeming quality and love the*
> *person for that."*
>
> (See QUOTATIONS, p. 51)

The family drives west in their Oldsmobile, which breaks down regularly and can't go over twenty-five miles per hour. They often take back roads to avoid tolls and sightsee. It takes them two months to get to Welch, West Virginia, deep in the Appalachian Mountains.

The family pulls up to an old house and meets Dad's mother, Erma, as well as Grandpa and Uncle Stanley. Uncle Stanley hugs and kisses Jeannette more than she would like. She thinks her relatives are strange and look nothing like Dad. The family sleeps in the basement, a dank, cinder block room with a coal stove and one bed for the kids to share.

When Mom takes the kids to enroll in school, she doesn't have their records but assures the principal that they are gifted. The principal makes the kids answer rapid-fire questions, but the children can't understand his Appalachian accent, and the principal can't

SUMMARY & ANALYSIS

understand them. The principal places them in remedial classes for students with learning disabilities.

In school, the kids struggle to assimilate. Jeannette cannot answer questions in history class the way she used to because the class focuses only on West Virginia. On the playground, a black girl named Dinitia Hewitt smiles at Jeannette, which Jeannette interprets as a friendly gesture until she realizes the smile is malicious. In English class, the teacher teases Jeannette for the incident in the principal's office, insinuating that she thinks she's superior to others. While the class laughs at Jeannette, Dinitia stabs her in the back with a pencil. For weeks, Dinitia and her friends beat up Jeannette at recess and make fun of her ragged clothing.

One day while walking in town, Jeannette comes across a small dog tormenting a little boy, and she helps the boy home piggyback. The boy happens to be Dinitia's neighbor, and Dinitia stops tormenting Jeannette. Soon, the girls start doing homework together, but Erma derides Jeannette for having a black friend. She blames the black people for Welch's decline. Eventually, Jeannette snaps and tells Erma not to use racial slurs. Erma calls her ungrateful and sends her to the basement without dinner. Mom tells Jeannette she has to be polite and show Erma compassion. Jeannette knows that they would be homeless without Erma and now understands that desperation breeds hypocrisy.

Mom and Dad go to Phoenix to retrieve the rest of their things. While they're away, Erma drinks often, hits the children with serving spoons, and tells them about her hard life as an orphan. One afternoon, Jeannette hears Brian crying and walks in on Erma molesting him. Jeannette and Lori confront Erma, which leads to a physical fight. Erma banishes them to the basement, not allowing them to eat or use the restroom. Uncle Stanley occasionally brings dinner, fearing Erma's wrath.

When Mom and Dad come back, Dad yells at the kids for disrespecting Erma and at Brian for being weak. Jeannette realizes that Erma must have done the same thing to Dad as a child. Erma banishes the whole family from her house, so the Wallses must find another place to live.

ANALYSIS

Life in Erma's house causes the Walls children to begin to rely on each other instead of their parents for safety. When Mom tells Jeannette not to challenge Erma's racism, Jeannette realizes that her parents will bend their strong values for survival. Although both Mom and Dad had previously been outspoken about their beliefs, because they now rely on Erma for shelter, they ignore their convictions in favor of practicality. However, Lori hugs Jeannette for speaking out against Erma's racist rants, demonstrating that Lori will support Jeannette's beliefs even when Mom won't. When Mom and Dad take the trip to Phoenix, Brian questions whether they'll return, demonstrating a further lack of faith in their parents. The children's dedication to each other comes to a head when Erma molests Brian. Not only do Lori and Jeannette intervene, but they refuse to back down when Dad admonishes them for it. Mom and Dad make no effort to protect their children from Erma's abuse and hatred, signaling again that Jeannette and her siblings will have to be their own parents.

Erma's attack on Brian provides context for some of Dad's behavior, allowing Jeannette and the reader to understand him better. First, Erma's alcoholism indicates that the family has a genetic predisposition to addiction, or at least that Dad grew up with a constant example of alcoholism. Second, Erma's bitter anger and resentment suggests that Dad grew up without praise, perhaps explaining why he now surrounds himself with people willing to see him as a hero. Dad places blame for the attack on Brian's weakness, which suggests he blames himself for the abuse he suffered. His focus on weakness provides context for his bizarre focus and aggressive approach to courage. He has internalized the narrative that fighting back could have saved him. The children's realization that Erma likely molested Dad allows them to feel compassion for him, but unlike their parents, they protect each other from abuse. Even after Dad scolds Jeannette and Lori for defending Brian, they refuse to apologize or ignore what happened. Unlike Dad, who adopted some of Erma's abusive behaviors, the Walls children refuse to accept this treatment, suggesting that they may break this cycle of generational abuse.

Life in Welch challenges the Wallses' perception of themselves as exceptional. Used to the narrative of her children's brilliance, Mom assumes she can once again ignore the rules and demand that the school in Welch place her children in accelerated courses. The public humiliation Jeannette's teacher puts her through as a result demonstrates that Welch punishes people who believe they're special. Dinitia's gang specifically targets Jeannette for putting on airs. When the bullies emphasize that Jeannette's coat has no buttons, they drive home both the reality of Jeannette's poverty and that the people of Welch consider material possessions integral to superiority. Furthermore, the school doesn't see Jeannette's intelligence because they only acknowledge and value things that are concretely practical to life in Welch. The principal doesn't even consider that a difference in accent, not intelligence, might explain her difficulty in communicating with the Walls children, demonstrating that she doesn't think about life beyond Welch. Jeannette no longer excels in her history class because the curriculum focuses only on West Virginia instead of the country as a whole. Her whole life Jeannette has been taught to value unconventional thinking and imagination, but Welch only has room for the concrete and practical.

PART III: WELCH, CONTINUED (LITTLE HOBART STREET)

SUMMARY
Dad buys a very small, precariously built house on Little Hobart Street. Mom admonishes the kids to notice the positives about the house, but it has no heat or indoor plumbing. They usually can't afford to have the electricity turned on. Nevertheless, the house sits on a lot of land, and Dad promises to soon start construction on the Glass Castle.

Dad is rarely home despite not having a job in Welch. He says he is investigating the United Miners Workers labor union, though Jeannette doesn't quite believe him. In order to help Dad get started on the Glass Castle, Brian and Jeannette dig a large hole in the ground for the foundation. Over time, however, the family starts filling the pit with garbage because they can't afford the garbage collection fee. Jeannette tries to improve the front of their home by painting it yellow, but a cold snap comes in and freezes the can of paint before she can finish.

Most of the Wallses' neighbors on Little Hobart Street live on welfare. The Hall family, for example, has six middle-aged kids with severe mental disabilities. The oldest, Kenny Hall, has a crush on Jeannette, and the other neighborhood kids torment him for it. The Pastor family, helmed by the town's sex worker, Ginnie Sue Pastor, has nine children. Curious, Jeannette befriends Ginnie Sue's daughter, Kathy, and goes to their house for dinner. Jeannette notices that the Pastor kids look remarkably different from one another.

She impresses the Pastors with her ability to pick the meat from a chicken and with stories about Las Vegas and Phoenix. Jeannette enjoys her evening with the Pastors and concludes that sex work, at least, puts food on the table.

Violence is also very common in Welch. The Walls children regularly fight gangs of other kids who make fun of them for being so poor. One day, a classmate named Ernie Goad throws a rock through their window and makes fun of them for living in garbage. To retaliate, Brian and Jeannette fashion a catapult from a mattress and fire dozens of rocks down the mountain at dangerous speeds. When Ernie and his friends run away terrified, Jeannette and Brian celebrate in the street.

One night, Dad comes home drunk with several injuries, and Jeannette has to give him sutures by hand. After that, Dad starts disappearing for days at a time, claiming that he is developing the technology to burn coal more efficiently. Jeannette no longer believes him. Mom still occasionally receives lease money from her land in Texas, but it is hardly enough to survive. The family eats poorly and irregularly, sometimes having to resort to cat food or ham with maggots.

Brian and Jeannette begin foraging for food around their house, stealing from people's farms, and dumpster diving in order to survive. Their classmates make fun of them for being skinny and not having lunch at school. Maureen survives by making friends and going to their homes for dinner. Once, the kids catch Mom eating a Hershey bar under a blanket. Brian takes it from her and splits it into four pieces for the kids.

ANALYSIS

This section signals the end of many things, including the Glass Castle and Jeannette's confidence in Dad. Jeannette and Brian's attempt to help Dad build the Glass Castle by digging the foundation represents a last chance for Dad to follow through on his promises. When the family starts filling this hole with garbage because they can't afford the city's garbage collection fee, Jeannette can no longer ignore the emptiness and worthlessness of Dad's promises. Jeannette and her siblings follow the trend of earlier sections and band closer together, with the exception of Maureen. Jeannette and Brian resort to stealing and digging through the trash for food, which they share. We can compare Jeannette's response to this great disappointment to the lessons she learned from Dad's swimming lesson in the Hot Pot. As with the Hot Pot, Jeannette has realized that she can't afford to rely on Dad, but this but this time, the realization makes her angry and frustrated rather than grateful.

The contrast between the other poor families in Welch and the Walls family emphasizes that Mom and Dad's selfishness lies at the root of their problems. Dad's fanciful stories of exposing union corruption echo his earlier tales of heroics, but he can no longer charm his starving children. Mom's platitudes about seeing the positive in the house serve to hide her responsibility for the family's situation. By encouraging her children to think positively, Mom implies the children's attitude, not their desperate situation, causes their misery. This rhetoric allows her to ignore the severity of the family's problems and avoid putting in the work to solve them. Jeannette's observation of her neighbors makes her parents' culpability even clearer. Although some of the Wallses' neighbors face even greater challenges and poverty, they still manage to put food on the table and not live in filth. Jeannette's observation that Ginnie Sue Pastor feeds her children is a direct response to her mom's judgment of the women at the Green Lantern. Mom may view herself as better than a sex worker, but her philosophy and art don't make money. Throughout this section, Jeannette comes to the painful realization that her parents have chosen to starve their family.

As Jeannette grows older, we see her enact the positive lessons she's learned from her parents while rejecting their hurtful patterns. For example, Jeannette reveals herself to be uniquely compassionate and open-minded, like Mom teaches her to be. When some neighborhood girls try to recruit Jeannette into the Junior KKK, she declines. As Jeannette describes how often they fought other children in Welch, she considers the larger contributing factors that led to a culture a violence, including union uprisings, dangerous labor laws, multi-generational trauma, an assessment that is both astute and free of judgment. Her description here demonstrates Mom's belief that one must always consider the suffering of others before they react or judge. However, Jeannette rejects her Mom's belief that true compassion involves never setting boundaries. When other kids torment Kenny Hall, their mentally disabled, middle-aged neighbor, Jeannette shows him kindness, but she firmly tells him she doesn't date older men when he asks her out. Just as Jeannette and Lori's defense of Brian shows an end to accepting generational trauma, Jeannette here puts an end to her mother's toxic socialization around boundaries.

PART III: WELCH, CONTINUED (WINTER, SPRING, SUMMER)

SUMMARY

When winter comes, the family can't afford coal or wood for the stove. Even with a fire, the house cannot hold heat because it is not insulated. Eventually, the pipes freeze, and the kids can't bathe, leading to their classmates making fun of them for smelling bad. One day, Lori tries to use kerosene to make a better fire in the stove, but the fire explodes, and she burns her eyebrows, bangs, and thighs. Lori and Brian run to get snow to cool her burns. Lori's blisters sting so badly, using a blanket hurts.

Erma dies that winter, and Dad is visibly distraught. After the funeral, Lori says, "Ding dong the witch is dead," causing Dad to lose his temper and run away for four days. Erma's house burns down that same winter because Uncle Stanley fell asleep with a cigarette in his hand. Grandpa and Uncle Stanley move into a house with running water, so the kids start going over for baths. One day, when Jeannette is sitting next to Stanley, he starts masturbating and touching Jeannette's thigh. When Jeannette tells Mom what happened, Mom says that Stanley is lonely and that sexual assault is a matter of perception.

Spring rains bring flash floods and mudslides, and the house falls into further disrepair. When the family can no longer use the stairs to get to the bathroom, Mom buys a yellow bucket to use as a toilet. One day, Brian finds a diamond ring outside their house. When they show the ring to Mom, she says she needs it for her self-esteem and refuses to pawn it. At this point, the family is nearing starvation, and Jeannette begs Mom to leave Dad so they can sign up for welfare. Mom doesn't believe in welfare and refuses to get a divorce because it goes against her Catholic faith. She also refuses to get a job because it wouldn't leave her any time to work on her art.

Despite the summer's humidity, Jeannette avoids the local pool because of bullies. The swimming times are also unofficially segregated. One day, Dinitia invites her to come during the hours that black families swim. Jeannette hesitates, not wanting to create conflict, but finds she loves the good-natured locker room teasing as well as the clean feeling of the chlorine. That same afternoon, a man with child welfare services comes to the house and asks Jeannette about her parents. She tells him that both her parents work, and he'll have to come back when they're home. Afterward, Jeannette is furious because she is afraid she and her siblings will be separated.

Jeannette tells Mom about the child welfare visit, and Mom agrees to get a teaching job. Mom hates teaching and regularly refuses to go to work, but it still brings in money. To make extra cash, Jeannette starts babysitting, Brian does yardwork, and Lori runs a paper route. Even with the extra income, Dad still drains their money before the end of the month, and the children are picking food out of the trash again.

ANALYSIS

The fire that hurts Lori parallels the fire in Jeannette's first memory to demonstrate how far the family has deteriorated. When Jeannette accidentally sets herself on fire, she is behaving like a normal three-year-old, who requires adult supervision around stoves. However, Lori is old enough to understand fire safety, but still acts recklessly out of desperation. The family's poverty has worsened so much that not even a responsible person like Lori can reliably show prudence. Mom and Dad don't bring Lori to the hospital but instead force her to tough out the pain. This difference shows how uninterested Mom and Dad have become in parenting, lost in their self-absorption. Lori's injury doesn't halt or change the rhythm of daily life. This nonreaction reveals that the family now considers injury and misfortune a normal occurrence, barely worth remarking upon. Mom and Dad no longer encourage their children to fight back, as they did when praising Jeannette's fascination with flame. Rather, Lori must simply endure hardship and survive.

Mom's deflection of responsibility throughout this section reveals once and for all that she uses philosophy as an excuse to avoid blame. Although Mom's Catholicism usually involves the occasional attendance at Mass, she evokes the Church's stance on divorce as a reason why she can't leave Dad. This selective devotion suggests that Catholicism here functions as an excuse for not undergoing the massive emotional and logistical work it would take to leave Dad. She rejects the idea of welfare on principle, refusing to acknowledge that the moral high ground she takes in preaching "compassion" completely breaks down when she repeatedly fails to protect Jeannette from sexual predators. Therefore, we can start to read her call for Jeannette to have compassion here as a desire to avoid confrontation with Grandpa or Uncle Stanley, who currently offer their only source of running water. She co-opts the ring for her self-esteem despite having preached the value of anti-materialism to her children, again allowing them to starve for her temporary happiness. Again and again, Mom weaponizes philosophy in a way that absolves her of blame, justifying her self-indulgence.

Throughout this section, Jeannette takes parental levels of responsibility for the family, an important shift in her relationship with her parents. Despite not even being in high school, the children take on jobs and put the money toward food instead of luxuries. Jeannette takes an advanced level of initiative to find out what the family has to do in order to receive welfare, looking at money like an adult. Her suggestion that Mom leave Dad so that the family doesn't starve shows just how much she's matured. First, this plan confirms that Jeannette's childhood hero worship of Dad has completely waned. Second, she demonstrates a willingness to sacrifice that neither of her parents possess. Dad still favors Jeannette, and she still loves him, but she wants Mom to leave him as a means of survival. Jeannette's practicality and willpower in this section give us an inkling of how she will eventually make her way to New York.

Part III: Welch, continued (High School)

Summary

When Jeannette starts high school, Dinitia tells Jeannette that her mother's boyfriend has moved in. Later, she tells Jeannette she is pregnant. When Dinitia disappears, Jeannette hears that she stabbed her mother's boyfriend to death.

Jeannette is disappointed that boys don't like her. She describes herself as tall and pale with bright red hair and buck teeth. Jeannette works as a proofreader for the school newspaper, the *Maroon Wave*, and finds that she likes the professional, fast-paced atmosphere of a newsroom. The typesetter complains about the way Jeannette smells, so she starts taking baths at Uncle Stanley's again, making sure to keep a safe distance.

The following summer, Mom goes to a conference in Charleston to renew her teaching license. Lori goes to a summer camp for gifted high school students, and Jeannette is excited to take control of the family budget. But when Dad asks for money, she finds herself unable to tell him no.

To pay Jeannette back for the money he's used, he takes her to a bar, where he wins eighty dollars in a pool game against his friend Robbie. As part of the scheme to distract Robbie, Dad lets Robbie dance with Jeannette. After, Robbie takes Jeannette upstairs to his apartment, where he attempts to rape her. When Jeannette tells Dad that Robbie attacked her, Dad compares the incident to the time he threw Jeannette in the hot spring, knowing she'd figure out how to survive. He says they make a great team.

To make ends meet, Jeannette lies about her age to get a job at Becker's Jewel Box. She likes the work, but Mr. Becker sometimes touches her inappropriately. When Mr. Becker refuses to let Jeannette earn commission, she steals a watch but returns it a few days later because she's afraid of losing her job.

Lori returns from camp renewed and inspired to leave Welch as soon as possible. Mom returns from Charleston and announces she will quit her teaching job and dedicate all her time to art. Furious and fed up, Jeannette confronts her parents for not being more responsible. Dad whips her with a belt for her disrespect. Jeannette runs outside to clear her head and decides she will also leave Welch. She buys a piggy bank to help her and Lori save for a new life in New York City.

Lori, Jeannette, and Brian save all the money they earn from odd jobs around Welch. One day, Jeannette comes home to find her piggy bank slashed and all the money gone. Dad vehemently denies stealing it and then disappears for three days. In the end, Jeannette secures Lori a summer babysitting job with a bus ticket to New York City as part of the payment.

Lori thrives in New York City, and Jeannette decides she will leave that summer and finish her senior year there. Dad tries to convince her to stay by showing her the blueprints to the Glass Castle, but she is determined to leave. Mournfully, Dad walks Jeannette to the bus station.

ANALYSIS

Dinitia's plight underscores how racism and segregation enforce artificial divides between people who otherwise have a lot in common. Dinitia doesn't identify the father when she tells Jeannette she is pregnant, but she later goes to prison for stabbing her mother's boyfriend to death. Jeannette does not explicitly draw any conclusions, but the narration implies that Dinitia was raped by her mother's boyfriend. From this incident, we can see that Dinitia and Jeannette's families have quite a few similarities, including unsafe home environments, parents who put themselves before their children, and sexual violence. These parallels reveal that extreme poverty, regardless of its root causes, can have the same tragic consequences regardless of race. Furthermore, the town's strained race relations prevent the girls from becoming very close. Had they been able to confide in each other, they could have at the very least provided some solace in mutual understanding. In this way, racism isolates Dinitia and Jeannette, depriving them each of an ally.

Dad's use of Jeannette to distract Robbie marks another shift in their relationship because Dad no longer treats her as his child. Dad actively encourages Jeannette to flirt with Robbie, a marked contrast to his childhood lesson on pervert hunting. When Jeannette confronts Dad after her escape, he cites their trip to the Hot Pot, indicating that he intentionally subjected Jeannette to the threat of sexual violence with Robbie, convinced that she could protect herself. Dad's explanation perverts the lesson that Jeannette internalized at the Hot Pot when she was a little girl. At the Hot Pot, Dad promises that he only put her in danger so that she would learn to swim or grow and become independent. With Robbie, Dad threw her in the proverbial pool so that they could win eighty dollars. A clue to this change in attitude lies in the way Dad says that they're a team. This word choice shows that Dad now views Jeannette as his teammate, his equal, not his daughter whom he has a duty to protect.

Mom and Dad punish Jeannette for calling out their parenting skills because she directly challenges their authority, shattering the family narrative. When Dad whips Jeannette with a belt, it's the first time either parent has disciplined their kids, which shows us how deeply Jeannette's words have cut him. Throughout Jeannette's childhood and up until Welch, the Walls family has always described themselves as creative and brilliant and implied the children were lucky to have such wonderful parents. While their hardships in Welch have by now thoroughly shattered this illusion, Jeannette is the first to explicitly say so by accusing Mom and Dad of not acting like parents. She has not just called out Mom and Dad but completely broken through their self-images. Dad's response, to impose physical punishment, reveals that he believes acting like a parent involves holding the power over one's children, controlling them instead of guiding and protecting them.

Part IV: New York City (Arrival and Homelessness)

Summary

As Jeannette glimpses New York City's skyline, she worries what people will think of her. She meets Lori's friend Evan at the bus station, and they walk to Zum Zum, a German restaurant where Lori works as a waitress. Lori seems exuberant, and Jeannette finds that New Yorkers are friendlier and more helpful than they appear. That night, Jeannette moves into the women's hostel with Lori.

Jeannette gets a job at a busy fast food restaurant and enjoys its lively, hectic pace. She and Lori move into an apartment in South Bronx, and Jeannette is thrilled to have such amenities as indoor plumbing and a gas stove. Jeannette sometimes gets jumped in the neighborhood, but she fights back in order to avoid becoming a regular target. She lands an internship at a local Brooklyn newspaper, *The Phoenix*, and her high school accepts the hours as credit. The newspaper struggles to meet payroll, but Jeannette loves the work. When she graduates from high school, they hire her as a full-time reporter.

When Jeannette and Lori write to Brian, they find that conditions in Welch are getting worse. The house has fallen into further disrepair and Maureen has moved in with the neighbors. When Jeannette describes their life in New York City, Brian follows in Jeannette's footsteps and leaves before his senior year in high school.

At first, Jeannette doesn't want to go to college because she likes her job as a reporter for *The Phoenix*. She believes that her ability to learn on the fly and research concepts she doesn't know serves her better than formal education. Mike Armstrong, the editor-in-chief, assures her she can find a better job with a degree, and so she decides to go to Barnard College. Barnard is an expensive private school, but Jeannette puts herself through with the help of grants, loans, savings, and part-time jobs.

Jeannette enjoys creating her own life and grows to dread phone calls from her parents. On one phone call, she learns that Maureen fell through the porch steps and gashed her head open. When Maureen turns twelve, Lori buys her a bus ticket to New York City and becomes her primary caretaker. Dad accuses Lori of stealing his children.

Three years after Maureen's arrival, Mom and Dad move to New York City. They quickly fall behind on rent and are kicked out of a series of apartments. Brian and Lori try to take them in on different occasions, but Dad's drinking and Mom's messiness quickly make the situation untenable. Dad and Mom live out of their van for a little while, but when it is towed, they find themselves homeless.

Mom and Dad call from pay phones and update their children on their new homeless lifestyle. Mom says that being homeless is like an adventure. Jeannette considers dropping out of Barnard to support Mom and Dad, but Brian and Lori remind her they have other options. She starts seeing her parents in every homeless person and is generous with her money. In a social sciences class, Jeannette suggests that some homeless people choose to be homeless, eliciting anger from her professor.

ANALYSIS

As Jeannette works hard to establish her new life, we see the ways in which her unconventional upbringing actually prepared her for the challenges of New York City. Because of the many things Jeannette lacked in childhood, she starts her new life feeling grateful for amenities that most people take for granted, such as a working stove and indoor plumbing. Her experience with fighting in Welch helps her fend off neighborhood muggers, and her experience with hunger causes her to celebrate something as simple as a hectic fast food job. Jeannette spent most of her teen years strategizing and working multiple jobs to survive, which has given her the skills to find funding to attend Barnard, one of the most expensive schools in New York City. Furthermore, Jeannette's ability to thrive at *The Phoenix* comes from the self-reliance she has learned over the years. Instead of asking her superiors about concepts she doesn't understand, she looks them up on her own, displaying the kind of self-starter attitude that makes a good journalist. Although Jeannette's childhood hurt her in many ways, Jeannette's suffering also gave her an exceptional amount of strength.

Now that the Walls children have grown up, we see in a new way that Mom and Dad cannot take care of themselves. They repeatedly fail to maintain shelter for themselves, and their inability to maintain the van leads to them losing it. Even when Brian and Lori offer them shelter, Mom and Dad do not create a stable lifestyle for themselves because they refuse to plan and work to create a future for themselves. In comparison to their hardworking children, Mom and Dad act like teenagers, living without regard for the future. Mom emphasizes this childishness when she calls homelessness an adventure, because she clearly has not considered the long-term consequences of life on the street, such as surviving the winter. The new dynamic between the Walls children and their parents makes it evident that Mom and Dad have depended on their children's self-reliance. Their negligence stemmed not from malice, but a profound inability to create any sort of structure in their lives.

As Jeannette finds stability, she must reconcile her new life of comfort and security with her parents' continued poverty. Even though she left Welch in part to stop having to take responsibility for her parents, Jeannette considers dropping out of college to support them, demonstrating how difficult it is for her to absolve herself of their care. Significantly, it is Lori and Brian who convince Jeannette to stay in school, protecting her from falling back into a toxic dynamic just as they protected each other from abusive cycles in Welch. Jeannette's simultaneous compassion toward and anger at homeless people reflects her emotional turmoil over her parents. While she gives generously to the homeless people she encounters, symbolically expressing concern for her parents, she insists in one of her classes that homeless people may choose to be homeless. This statement expresses her frustration and anger at her parent's constant inaction throughout her childhood and their ambivalence regarding their current plight. She realizes that just as she cannot make them help her, she cannot force them to help themselves.

PART IV: NEW YORK CITY, CONTINUED (HOMELESS WINTER) & PART V: THANKSGIVING

SUMMARY: PART IV
When winter comes, Mom and Dad find homelessness more difficult. Dad stays in shelters, and Mom stays with Lori. When Dad gets tuberculosis, he spends six weeks recovering in the hospital, forcing him to get sober. A hospital administrator gets him a maintenance job at an upstate resort, but Mom doesn't want to go, so Dad goes by himself. He enjoys his time near the woods and stays sober through the summer and fall. Mom convinces him to come back the next winter, and he immediately returns to drinking.

That Christmas, Jeannette buys Dad warm clothes for the winter, and he is offended that she would treat him like a charity case. When Jeannette can't afford her tuition fees the following semester, Dad goes out and wins $950 and a mink coat in a poker game to cover the cost. When she graduates, she does not invite him to the ceremony because she worries he will show up drunk and cause a scene. Dad understands and still expresses pride in her success.

Mom and Dad move into an abandoned building in the Lower East Side, living with other squatters who have led unruly lives and battled authority. Jeannette observes that her parents have found their home, the place they belong, and wonders if she will ever find the same.

In her search for home, Jeannette begins dating a man named Eric. She likes Eric because he is organized, responsible, and nothing like her father. They quickly move in together, and Jeannette gets a job writing gossip articles for a prestigious news outlet. Dad occasionally calls in tips for her column. Jeannette enjoys going to fancy parties, but she fears people will find out about her parents and her past.

Four years later, when Jeannette and Eric are married, Mom asks Jeannette to borrow a million dollars from him. Mom wants the money to buy her brother's oil-rich property, which is identical to the property Mom inherited. Jeannette realizes that Mom's property is also worth the same amount of money, and that Mom sat on a million-dollar property while the family starved.

At this point, Jeannette is a successful journalist, Lori is a freelance artist, and Brian is a police officer with a wife and a child. Maureen drops out of community college and moves in with Mom and Dad. Maureen behaves erratically, and one day tries to stab Mom. She spends a year in a mental institution and moves to California when she's released. The family drifts apart, and a year later Dad dies of a heart attack. Jeannette sees Dad once before his death. They reminisce about old times, and Jeannette concludes that he loves her. A year after Dad dies, Jeannette divorces Eric and moves into an apartment on the West Side.

SUMMARY: PART V

Five years after Dad dies, Jeannette and her new husband, John, host the family for Thanksgiving dinner. John is a writer who admires Jeannette's strength and says her scars prove that she is strong. Brian is a decorated sergeant and recently divorced, and Lori is an illustrator.

The family eats a large meal, and Brian notes that if someone is determined to put food on the table, they will find a way to do it. Jeannette often has similar thoughts on seeing abundant amounts of food. Lori admonishes him for bringing up the past, but the conversation remains good-natured. Sitting down for dinner, they all toast to Dad's life.

ANALYSIS

As Jeannette, Lori, and Brian appear to grow into well-adjusted adults, Mom, Dad, and Maureen struggle to adapt to life in New York City, highlighting their lack of independence. Mom and Dad's unique struggles on the streets of New York City highlight their toxic dynamic. Away from Mom, Dad manages to stay sober for nearly half a year, but when he comes back, he returns to his old habits and behavior. Mom can't be blamed for Dad's alcoholism, but the two of them do appear to bring out the worst in each other. Jeannette supposes that Maureen's inability to establish independence in New York City could be attributed to the fact that she survived in Welch by relying on others, unlike her siblings who learned to fend for themselves. Her mental deterioration later in life reveals one of the many flaws in Mom and Dad's extreme parenting style. As the youngest child, Maureen grew up during the most turbulent episodes the Walls family went through, which meant she got the least functional and least present versions of Mom and Dad as her guides. Unlike her siblings, Maureen never received the tools she needed to thrive.

Toward the end of his life, Dad appears to regret his loss of connection with Jeannette and attempts to make amends in his own way. His anger at receiving warm clothes for Christmas demonstrates that Jeannette's care for him hurts his pride. In light of this, we can see his contribution to Jeannette's college tuition as an attempt to restore balance in their relationship by, for once, providing for Jeannette's education. His understanding that Jeannette might not want him at graduation demonstrates an unprecedented humility and suggests that he now is willing to put Jeannette's feelings before his own. Although they never truly reconcile, Jeannette and Dad manage to forge a kind of relationship before his death through Dad's interest in her journalism career. These small steps allow Jeannette to remember what she once loved about Dad, making it possible for her to agree with John's toast at the end.

As Jeannette becomes more secure in her new life, she begins to reach a place of understanding with her parents and even finds herself able to learn from them. When Mom and Dad become squatters on Manhattan's Lower East Side, she recognizes that they found purpose and a place to belong. Jeannette notices that while her parents' life as squatters allows them to live in accordance with their true selves, her life, while comfortable, forces her to deny her roots. She keeps her past hidden from her colleagues, fearing that she would lose her job if people found out about her parents. After Dad dies, Jeannette grows restless and unsatisfied, divorces her husband, and moves to a different part of town, indicating that she realizes she has not yet truly found the home she was searching for with Eric in New York City. When Jeannette and her second husband, John, host the family for Thanksgiving dinner five years later, it appears Jeannette has found her true home. John states that he views her scar as a sign of her strength, symbolizing his acceptance of and appreciation for everything Jeannette endured to become the person she is now.

IMPORTANT QUOTATIONS EXPLAINED

1.   *I wondered if the fire were out to get me. I wondered if all*
      fire was related, like Dad said all humans were related . . .
      I didn't have the answers to those questions, but what I did
      know was that I lived in a world that at any moment could
      erupt into fire.

This quotation, which appears in Part II after the hotel in San
Francisco catches fire, marks the first time Jeannette realizes that
her life, although still exciting in her eyes, also has a threatening
quality. At only four years old, Jeannette has encountered an inor-
dinate number of fires, the first one landing her in the hospital for
weeks. Although these fires are not related in any ancestral sense, as
she supposes in the quote, they do share a common denominator:
her parents' negligence. Mom and Dad frequently leave her unat-
tended with stoves and matches, and even encourage her to play
with matches after her hospital stay. Jeannette displaces blame for
the danger in her life on the fire itself instead of her parents because
she still views Mom and Dad as heroic figures in her life. Jeannette's
understanding of the danger in her life as unpredictable, something
that could happen at any time, underscores the lack of stability her
parents offer her. Her world can change in an instant, catching on
fire, because of her family's nomadic and reckless lifestyle.

2.   *Maybe I should have cut him some slack. With his broken*
      wing and a lifetime of eating roadkill, he probably had a lot
      to be ungrateful about. Too much hard luck can create
      a permanent meanness of spirit in any creature.

In this quote, Jeannette describes Buster, their old pet buzzard in
Battle Mountain, whom Jeannette found intolerable and ungrateful. Her reflection about the way a difficult life can change a being
for the worse is an early manifestation of the theme of how trauma
has long-range effects. Buster has a lot in common with Erma,
Dad's mother, whose cruel treatment of her grandchildren certainly

49

shows a meanness of spirit. We learn that Erma was orphaned at a young age and shipped off to various relatives who mistreated her throughout childhood, and this "hard luck" made her mean and abusive. This pattern also appears in Welch as a whole, which Jeannette describes as a violent town. The miners constantly struggle for financial stability, leading to anger that they take out on their families. While Jeannette herself does not appear to develop a meanness of spirit, her ability to fight off muggers in New York shows a toughness that her hard life gave her.

3.   *Dad told us that zone was known in physics as the boundary between turbulence and order. "It's the place where no rules apply, or at least they haven't figured 'em out yet," he said. "You-all got a little too close to it today."*

Dad makes this comment to Jeannette and Brian after they set a batch of hazardous waste on fire, and Brian nearly burns to death. Here, Dad refers both to the physics of the hazy area that manifests over a flame, and also suggests that Brian and Jeannette were too reckless. Dad's quiet and grave tone may indicate that he's too thankful they survived to be angry, but it could also suggest a moment of self-reflection, as Dad intentionally subjects his kids to a life of chaos and lawlessness, not unlike the boundary between turbulence and order. Traditionally, parents guide and discipline their children to help them navigate the physical, legal, and social rules of the greater world. Mom and Dad, on the other hand, allow their children to discover the world without much direction or supervision. In this quotation, Dad sees that this philosophy almost cost Jeannette and Brian their lives.

4.   *I could hear people around us whispering about the crazy drunk man and his dirty little urchin children, but who cared what they thought? None of them had ever had their hand licked by a cheetah.*

This quotation takes place as a police officer escorts the Walls family out of the Phoenix Zoo after Dad breaks into the cheetah's cage. Jeannette's lack of embarrassment at the gossiping onlookers shows that she has come to adopt her father's belief that exceptional people don't have to play by the rules. At this point in her childhood, Jeannette rationalizes that her life differs from other children's lives because her family is more special than others. Notably, Jeannette doesn't notice people's fear for her safety, which we can assume comprised part of the spectators' reaction, and instead focuses on their negative assessment of her and her father. This omission shows that Jeannette cannot even consider the possibility that her father would put her in danger. Her retorting comment about the cheetah suggests that she finds their comments petty, perhaps even jealous.

5.   *"You should never hate anyone, even your worst enemies. Everyone has something good about them. You have to find the redeeming quality and love the person for that."*

Mom says this quote to Jeannette after Jeannette admonishes Erma for her racist language and attitudes. This quotation encapsulates Mom's belief that everyone deserves compassion regardless of their behavior, a philosophy that has the potential to put the feelings of others above personal safety. For example, Mom extends compassion and understanding to Dad's reckless alcoholic behavior despite the pain he causes her and the danger he puts both her and their children in. She later encourages Jeannette to allow Uncle Stanley to molest her simply because he is lonely, again asserting that trauma and pain entitle people to hurt others. In this way, Mom equates setting healthy and protective boundaries with lacking empathy. This philosophy allows Mom to avoid confrontation with the many people who hurt Jeannette throughout the novel and also justify her own selfishness. Mom describes herself as an "excitement addict," meaning that the children must therefore accept her shortcomings just as they excuse Dad's alcohol addiction. As Jeannette grows older, she learns how to practice empathy and compassion without sacrificing her wellbeing.

QUOTATIONS

KEY FACTS

FULL TITLE
  The Glass Castle: A Memoir

AUTHOR
  Jeannette Walls

TYPE OF WORK
  Memoir

GENRE
  Bildungsroman, memoir, creative nonfiction

LANGUAGE
  English

TIME AND PLACE WRITTEN
  Early 2000s, New York

DATE OF FIRST PUBLICATION
  March 2005

PUBLISHER
  Simon & Schuster

NARRATOR
  Jeannette Walls narrates the details of her childhood.

POINT OF VIEW
  Jeannette Walls narrates in the first person, describing the
  events of her childhood. She focuses on her thoughts and
  emotions at the time instead of offering insight and analysis
  from her adult self.

TONE
  Observational, matter-of-fact, detached

TENSE
  Past

SETTING (TIME)
  Early 1960s to 2000

SETTING (PLACE)
>   Across the American Southwest; San Francisco; Welch, West
>   Virginia; New York City

PROTAGONIST
>   Jeannette Walls

MAJOR CONFLICT
>   As Jeannette struggles with her complicated feelings toward
>   Mom and Dad, she must also survive and adapt to the extreme
>   situations their recklessness places her in.

RISING ACTION
>   Mom and Dad's ambivalence repeatedly places Jeannette and
>   her three siblings at risk of starvation, serious physical injury,
>   sexual assault, and hypothermia. Dad dazzles the children
>   by framing their lifestyle as exciting and adventurous, but
>   the children slowly realize, in their own time, that they are in
>   danger and that Dad's promises of a better life are empty.

CLIMAX
>   Jeannette finally confronts her parents about not taking better
>   care of them and refuses to apologize. This moment crystallizes
>   Jeannette's realization that her parents will never take care of
>   her and cements her desire to escape.

FALLING ACTION
>   Dad whips Jeannette with a belt for disrespecting him. Outraged
>   and fed up, Jeannette decides that she will leave Welch as soon
>   as she can. Soon after, Jeannette and Lori make concrete plans to
>   leave for New York City and eventually follow through. Brian
>   and Maureen later join them, and then Mom and Dad arrive.
>   Dad dies after about ten years in New York.

THEMES
>   Strength from hardship, compassion versus boundaries, abuse

MOTIFS
>   Fire, animals, hypocrisy

SYMBOLS
>   The Glass Castle, stars, the Joshua tree

KEY FACTS

FORESHADOWING

When Dad and Jeannette pretend to go Demon Hunting, this foreshadows when they will go "Pervert Hunting" after Jeannette is molested in Phoenix.

Jeannette thinks Uncle Stanley is too touchy-feely when they first meet, which foreshadows him molesting her a couple years later.

STUDY QUESTIONS

1.   *The memoir opens with a scene from Jeannette's adulthood in New York City, rather than with her first memory. What effect does this structure have on the narrative? What effect does this have on your interpretation of the characters?*

The opening scene removes some of the tension from the memoir by promising a somewhat happy ending for Jeannette. While we read about Jeannette's turbulent and impoverished childhood, we don't have to wonder whether or not these experiences will stunt her later in life. We know, from the beginning, that Jeannette will eventually live in a nice apartment in New York City and have enough money to help Mom and Dad. By removing the question of her ultimate comfort and safety, Jeannette allows the memoir to focus on the family's interpersonal dynamics, how their relationships changed over time, and how these changes led to the family living such vastly different lives in New York City. Furthermore, Jeannette's conversation with Mom in the restaurant, however frustrating, casts Mom in a somewhat sympathetic light. No matter how egregious Mom's negligence becomes, we read each scene with the image of her picking through the dumpster.

2.   *After Erma molests Brian, Lori and Jeannette confront and physically attack Erma. What is the significance of this event?*

When Jeannette and Lori attack Erma for molesting Brian, they reveal both a source of their generational trauma and the limits to their parents' protection. In their defense of Brian, Jeannette and Lori make use of the lessons their parents taught them. Jeannette calls Erma a pervert, evoking Dad's "Pervert Hunting" expedition from Phoenix and identifying her as a threat. She and Lori respond to Erma's threat with aggression, showing Erma they're not afraid, exactly as Dad always taught them to do in the face of a predator. By both taking Erma's side and condemning his children for following his teachings, Dad reveals himself to be a hypocrite. Dad clearly has not grown past his trauma, as evidenced by his unwillingness to listen to Jeannette's explanations and by blaming Brian's weakness. Jeannette notes that Dad's trauma makes his behavior make sense, but at Lori's suggestion she drops the subject from her mind. Her willingness not to explore farther or talk to Dad demonstrates a rift between them, meaning that she realizes she cannot rely on him to protect the family from Erma.

3.   *What is the significance of Mom and Dad's home with the squatters on the Lower East Side of Manhattan?*

Jeannette's visit to her parents' apartment causes her to reassess what home means to her. When she first visits Mom and Dad in their squatters' apartment, she finds a building filled with other people who have lived according to extreme, nonconformist values, often running from authority and structure. These people are kindred spirits to Mom and Dad and embrace them in their community. Jeannette then realizes that Mom and Dad have found their true home in a way that she has not. Though she has in many ways established the comfortable, structured life she always wanted, it doesn't yet provide her with the sense of belonging that Mom and Dad have found as squatters. When she moves into her boyfriend Eric's apartment, she has to remind herself she belongs there, because she finds the opulence overwhelming. She often lies to the people she meets at parties about her upbringing because she fears their disdain if they knew the truth. Mom and Dad's apartment demonstrates to Jeannette that home involves not just stability but also an honest acceptance of who you are.

How to Write Literary Analysis

The Literary Essay: A Step-by-Step Guide

When you read for pleasure, your only goal is enjoyment. You might find yourself reading to get caught up in an exciting story, to learn about an interesting time or place, or just to pass time. Maybe you're looking for inspiration, guidance, or a reflection of your own life. There are as many different, valid ways of reading a book as there are books in the world.

When you read a work of literature in an English class, however, you're being asked to read in a special way: you're being asked to perform *literary analysis*. To analyze something means to break it down into smaller parts and then examine how those parts work, both individually and together. Literary analysis involves examining all the parts of a novel, play, short story, or poem—elements such as character, setting, tone, and imagery—and thinking about how the author uses those elements to create certain effects.

A literary essay isn't a book review: you're not being asked whether or not you liked a book or whether you'd recommend it to another reader. A literary essay also isn't like the kind of book report you wrote when you were younger, when your teacher wanted you to summarize the book's action. A high school or college–level literary essay asks, "How does this piece of literature actually work?" "How does it do what it does?" and, "Why might the author have made the choices he or she did?"

The Seven Steps
No one is born knowing how to analyze literature; it's a skill and a process you can master. As you gain more practice with this kind of thinking and writing, you'll be able to craft a method that works best for you. But until then, here are seven basic steps to writing a well-constructed literary essay:

> *1. Ask questions*
> *2. Collect evidence*
> *3. Construct a thesis*

4. Develop and organize arguments
5. Write the introduction
6. Write the body paragraphs
7. Write the conclusion

---

1. Ask Questions

When you're assigned a literary essay in class, your teacher will often provide you with a list of writing prompts. Lucky you! Now all you have to do is choose one. Do yourself a favor and pick a topic that interests you. You'll have a much better (not to mention easier) time if you start off with something you enjoy thinking about. If you are asked to come up with a topic by yourself, though, you might start to feel a little panicked. Maybe you have too many ideas—or none at all. Don't worry. Take a deep breath and start by asking yourself these questions:

- **What struck you?** Did a particular image, line, or scene linger in your mind for a long time? If it fascinated you, chances are you can draw on it to write a fascinating essay.

- **What confused you?** Maybe you were surprised to see a character act in a certain way, or maybe you didn't understand why the book ended the way it did. Confusing moments in a work of literature are like a loose thread in a sweater: if you pull on it, you can unravel the entire thing. Ask yourself why the author chose to write about that character or scene the way he or she did, and you might tap into some important insights about the work as a whole.

- **Did you notice any patterns?** Is there a phrase that the main character uses constantly or an image that repeats throughout the book? If you can figure out how that pattern weaves through the work and what the significance of that pattern is, you've almost got your entire essay mapped out.

- **Did you notice any contradictions or ironies?** Great works of literature are complex; great literary essays recognize and explain those complexities. Maybe the title of the work seems to contradict its content (for example, the play *Happy Days* shows its two characters buried up to their waists in dirt). Maybe the main character acts one way around his or her family and a completely different way around his or her friends and associates. If you can find a way to explain a work's contradictory elements, you've got the seeds of a great essay.

At this point, you don't need to know exactly what you're going to say about your topic; you just need a place to begin your exploration. You can help direct your reading and brainstorming by formulating your topic as a *question*, which you'll then try to answer in your essay. The best questions invite critical debates and discussions, not just a rehashing of the summary. Remember, you're looking for something you can *prove or argue* based on evidence you find in the text. Finally, remember to keep the scope of your question in mind: is this a topic you can adequately address within the word or page limit you've been given? Conversely, is this a topic big enough to fill the required length?

GOOD QUESTIONS

> *"Are Romeo and Juliet's parents responsible for the deaths of their children?"*
> *"Why do pigs keep showing up in* Lord of the Flies*?"*
> *"Are Dr. Frankenstein and his monster alike? How?"*

BAD QUESTIONS

> *"What happens to Scout in* To Kill a Mockingbird*?"*
> *"What do the other characters in* Julius Caesar *think about Caesar?"*
> *"How does Hester Prynne in* The Scarlet Letter *remind me of my sister?"*

---

2. COLLECT EVIDENCE

Once you know what question you want to answer, it's time to scour the book for things that will help you answer the question. Don't worry if you don't know what you want to say yet—right now you're just collecting ideas and material and letting it all percolate. Keep track of passages, symbols, images, or scenes that deal with your topic. Eventually, you'll start making connections between these examples, and your thesis will emerge.

Here's a brief summary of the various parts that compose each and every work of literature. These are the elements that you will analyze in your essay and that you will offer as evidence to support your arguments. For more on the parts of literary works, see the Glossary of Literary Terms at the end of this section.

ELEMENTS OF STORY   These are the *what*s of the work—what happens, where it happens, and to whom it happens.

- **Plot:** All the events and actions of the work.

- **Character:** The people who act and are acted on in a literary work. The main character of a work is known as the *protagonist*.

- **Conflict:** The central tension in the work. In most cases, the protagonist wants something, while opposing forces (antagonists) hinder the protagonist's progress.

- **Setting:** When and where the work takes place. Elements of setting include location, time period, time of day, weather, social atmosphere, and economic conditions.

- **Narrator:** The person telling the story. The narrator may straightforwardly report what happens, convey the subjective opinions and perceptions of one or more characters, or provide commentary and opinion in his or her own voice.

- **Themes:** The main idea or message of the work—usually an abstract idea about people, society, or life in general. A work may have many themes, which may be in tension with one another.

ELEMENTS OF STYLE These are the *how*s—how the characters speak, how the story is constructed, and how language is used throughout the work.

- **Structure and organization:** How the parts of the work are assembled. Some novels are narrated in a linear, chronological fashion, while others skip around in time. Some plays follow a traditional three- or five-act structure, while others are a series of loosely connected scenes. Some authors deliberately leave gaps in their work, leaving readers to puzzle out the missing information. A work's structure and organization can tell you a lot about the kind of message it wants to convey.

- **Point of view:** The perspective from which a story is told. In *first-person point of view*, the narrator involves himself or herself in the story. ("I went to the store"; "We watched in horror as the bird slammed into the window.") A first-person narrator is usually the protagonist of the work, but not always. In *third-person point of view*, the narrator does not participate

LITERARY ANALYSIS

in the story. A third-person narrator may closely follow a specific character, recounting that individual character's thoughts or experiences, or it may be what we call an *omniscient* narrator. Omniscient narrators see and know all: they can witness any event in any time or place and are privy to the inner thoughts and feelings of all characters. Remember that the narrator and the author are not the same thing!

- **Diction:** Word choice. Whether a character uses dry, clinical language or flowery prose with lots of exclamation points can tell you a lot about his or her attitude and personality.

- **Syntax:** Word order and sentence construction. Syntax is a crucial part of establishing an author's narrative voice. Ernest Hemingway, for example, is known for writing in very short, straightforward sentences, while James Joyce characteristically wrote in long, extremely complicated lines.

- **Tone:** The mood or feeling of the text. Diction and syntax often contribute to the tone of a work. A novel written in short, clipped sentences that use small, simple words might feel brusque, cold, or matter-of-fact.

- **Imagery:** Language that appeals to the senses, representing things that can be seen, smelled, heard, tasted, or touched.

- **Figurative language:** Language that is not meant to be interpreted literally. The most common types of figurative language are *metaphors* and *similes*, which compare two unlike things in order to suggest a similarity between them— for example, "All the world's a stage," or "The moon is like a ball of green cheese." (Metaphors say one thing *is* another thing; similes claim that one thing is *like* another thing.)

---

3. CONSTRUCT A THESIS

When you've examined all the evidence you've collected and know how you want to answer the question, it's time to write your thesis statement. A *thesis* is a claim about a work of literature that needs to be supported by evidence and arguments. The thesis statement is the heart of the literary essay, and the bulk of your paper will be spent trying to prove this claim. A good thesis will be:

- **Arguable.** "*The Great Gatsby* describes New York society in the 1920s" isn't a thesis—it's a fact.

- **Provable through textual evidence.** "*Hamlet* is a confusing but ultimately very well-written play" is a weak thesis because it offers the writer's personal opinion about the book. Yes, it's arguable, but it's not a claim that can be proved or supported with examples taken from the play itself.

- **Surprising.** "Both George and Lenny change a great deal in *Of Mice and Men*" is a weak thesis because it's obvious. A really strong thesis will argue for a reading of the text that is not immediately apparent.

- **Specific.** "Dr. Frankenstein's monster tells us a lot about the human condition" is *almost* a really great thesis statement, but it's still too vague. What does the writer mean by "a lot"? *How* does the monster tell us so much about the human condition?

GOOD THESIS STATEMENTS

Question: In *Romeo and Juliet*, which is more powerful in shaping the lovers' story: fate or foolishness?

Thesis: "Though Shakespeare defines Romeo and Juliet as 'star-crossed lovers,' and images of stars and planets appear throughout the play, a closer examination of that celestial imagery reveals that the stars are merely witnesses to the characters' foolish activities and not the causes themselves."

Question: How does the bell jar function as a symbol in Sylvia Plath's *The Bell Jar*?

Thesis: "A bell jar is a bell-shaped glass that has three basic uses: to hold a specimen for observation, to contain gases, and to maintain a vacuum. The bell jar appears in each of these capacities in *The Bell Jar*, Plath's semi-autobiographical novel, and each appearance marks a different stage in Esther's mental breakdown."

Question: Would Piggy in *The Lord of the Flies* make a good island leader if he were given the chance?

Thesis: "Though the intelligent, rational, and innovative Piggy has the mental characteristics of a good leader, he ultimately lacks the social skills necessary to be an effective one. Golding emphasizes this point by giving Piggy a foil in the charismatic Jack, whose magnetic personality allows him to capture and wield power effectively, if not always wisely."

4. Develop and Organize Arguments

The reasons and examples that support your thesis will form the middle paragraphs of your essay. Since you can't really write your thesis statement until you know how you'll structure your argument, you'll probably end up working on steps 3 and 4 at the same time. There's no single method of argumentation that will work in every context. One essay prompt might ask you to compare and contrast two characters, while another asks you to trace an image through a given work of literature. These questions require different kinds of answers and therefore different kinds of arguments. Below, we'll discuss three common kinds of essay prompts and some strategies for constructing a solid, well-argued case.

Types of Literary Essays

- **Compare and contrast**

  Compare and contrast the characters of Huck and Jim in The Adventures of Huckleberry Finn.

  Chances are you've written this kind of essay before. In an academic literary context, you'll organize your arguments the same way you would in any other class. You can either go *subject by subject* or *point by point*. In the former, you'll discuss one character first and then the second. In the latter, you'll choose several traits (attitude toward life, social status, images and metaphors associated with the character) and devote a paragraph to each. You may want to use a mix of these two approaches—for example, you may want to spend a paragraph apiece broadly sketching Huck's and Jim's personalities before transitioning to a paragraph or two describing a few key points of comparison. This can be a highly effective strategy if you want to make a counterintuitive argument—that, despite seeming to be totally different, the two characters or objects being compared are actually similar in a very important way (or vice versa). Remember that your essay should reveal something fresh or unexpected about the text, so think beyond the obvious parallels and differences.

- **Trace**

  Choose an image—for example, birds, knives, or eyes—and trace that image throughout Macbeth.

Sounds pretty easy, right? All you need to do is read the play, underline every appearance of a knife in *Macbeth* and then list them in your essay in the order they appear, right? Well, not exactly. Your teacher doesn't want a simple catalog of examples. He or she wants to see you make *connections* between those examples—that's the difference between summarizing and analyzing. In the *Macbeth* example, think about the different contexts in which knives appear in the play and to what effect. In *Macbeth*, there are real knives and imagined knives; knives that kill and knives that simply threaten. Categorize and classify your examples to give them some order. Finally, always keep the overall effect in mind. After you choose and analyze your examples, you should come to some greater understanding about the work, as well as the role of your chosen image, symbol, or phrase in developing the major themes and stylistic strategies of that work.

- **Debate**

  Is the society depicted in 1984 *good for its citizens?*

In this kind of essay, you're being asked to debate a moral, ethical, or aesthetic issue regarding the work. You might be asked to judge a character or group of characters *(Is Caesar responsible for his own demise?)* or the work itself *(Is* Jane Eyre *a feminist novel?)*. For this kind of essay, there are two important points to keep in mind. First, don't simply base your arguments on your personal feelings and reactions. Every literary essay expects you to read and analyze the work, so search for evidence in the text. What do characters in *1984* have to say about the government of Oceania? What images does Orwell use that might give you a hint about his attitude toward the government? As in any debate, you also need to make sure that you define all the necessary terms before you begin to argue your case. What does it mean to be a "good" society? What makes a novel "feminist"? You should define your terms right up front, in the first paragraph after your introduction.

LITERARY ANALYSIS

Second, remember that strong literary essays make contrary and surprising arguments. Try to think outside the box. In the *1984* example above, it seems like the obvious answer would be no, the totalitarian society depicted in Orwell's novel is *not* good for its citizens. But can you think of any arguments for the opposite side? Even if your final assertion is that the novel depicts a cruel, repressive, and therefore harmful society, acknowledging and responding to the counterargument will strengthen your overall case.

---

5. WRITE THE INTRODUCTION

Your introduction sets up the entire essay. It's where you present your topic and articulate the particular issues and questions you'll be addressing. It's also where you, as the writer, introduce yourself to your readers. A persuasive literary essay immediately establishes its writer as a knowledgeable, authoritative figure.

An introduction can vary in length depending on the overall length of the essay, but in a traditional five-paragraph essay it should be no longer than one paragraph. However long it is, your introduction needs to:

- **Provide any necessary context.** Your introduction should situate the reader and let him or her know what to expect. What book are you discussing? Which characters? What topic will you be addressing?

- **Answer the "So what?" question.** Why is this topic important, and why is your particular position on the topic noteworthy? Ideally, your introduction should pique the reader's interest by suggesting how your argument is surprising or otherwise counterintuitive. Literary essays make unexpected connections and reveal less-than-obvious truths.

- **Present your thesis.** This usually happens at or very near the end of your introduction.

- **Indicate the shape of the essay to come.** Your reader should finish reading your introduction with a good sense of the scope of your essay as well as the path you'll take toward proving your thesis. You don't need to spell out every step, but you do need to suggest the organizational pattern you'll be using.

Your introduction should not:

- **Be vague.** Beware of the two killer words in literary analysis: *interesting* and *important*. Of course, the work, question, or example is interesting and important—that's why you're writing about it!

- **Open with any grandiose assertions.** Many student readers think that beginning their essays with a flamboyant statement, such as "Since the dawn of time, writers have been fascinated by the topic of free will," makes them sound important and commanding. In fact, it sounds pretty amateurish.

- **Wildly praise the work.** Another typical mistake student writers make is extolling the work or author. Your teacher doesn't need to be told that "Shakespeare is perhaps the greatest writer in the English language." You can mention a work's reputation in passing—by referring to *The Adventures of Huckleberry Finn* as "Mark Twain's enduring classic," for example—but don't make a point of bringing it up unless that reputation is key to your argument.

- **Go off-topic.** Keep your introduction streamlined and to the point. Don't feel the need to throw in all kinds of bells and whistles in order to impress your reader—just get to the point as quickly as you can, without skimping on any of the required steps.

---

6. Write the Body Paragraphs

Once you've written your introduction, you'll take the arguments you developed in step 4 and turn them into your body paragraphs. The organization of this middle section of your essay will largely be determined by the argumentative strategy you use, but no matter how you arrange your thoughts, your body paragraphs need to do the following:

- **Begin with a strong topic sentence.** Topic sentences are like signs on a highway: they tell the readers where they are and where they're going. A good topic sentence not only alerts readers to what issue will be discussed in the following paragraphs but also gives them a sense of what argument will be made *about* that issue. "Rumor and gossip play an important role in *The Crucible*" isn't a strong topic sentence because it doesn't tell us very much. "The community's constant gossiping creates an environment that allows false accusations to flourish" is a much stronger topic sentence—

it not only tells us what the paragraph will discuss (gossip) but how the paragraph will discuss the topic (by showing how gossip creates a set of conditions that leads to the play's climactic action).

- **Fully and completely develop a single thought.** Don't skip around in your paragraph or try to stuff in too much material. Body paragraphs are like bricks: each individual one needs to be strong and sturdy or the entire structure will collapse. Make sure you have really proven your point before moving on to the next one.

- **Use transitions effectively.** Good literary essay writers know that each paragraph must be clearly and strongly linked to the material around it. Think of each paragraph as a response to the one that precedes it. Use transition words and phrases such as *however*, *similarly*, *on the contrary*, *therefore*, and *furthermore* to indicate what kind of response you're making.

---

7. Write the Conclusion

Just as you used the introduction to ground your readers in the topic before providing your thesis, you'll use the conclusion to quickly summarize the specifics learned thus far and then hint at the broader implications of your topic. A good conclusion will:

- **Do more than simply restate the thesis.** If your thesis argued that *The Catcher in the Rye* can be read as a Christian allegory, don't simply end your essay by saying, "And that is why *The Catcher in the Rye* can be read as a Christian allegory." If you've constructed your arguments well, this kind of statement will just be redundant.

- **Synthesize the arguments rather than summarizing them.** Similarly, don't repeat the details of your body paragraphs in your conclusion. The readers have already read your essay, and chances are it's not so long that they've forgotten all your points by now.

- **Revisit the "So what?" question.** In your introduction, you made a case for why your topic and position are important. You should close your essay with the same sort of gesture. What do your readers know now that they didn't know before? How will that knowledge help them better appreciate or understand the work overall?

- **Move from the specific to the general.** Your essay has most likely treated a very specific element of the work—a single character, a small set of images, or a particular passage. In your conclusion, try to show how this narrow discussion has wider implications for the work overall. If your essay on *To Kill a Mockingbird* focused on the character of Boo Radley, for example, you might want to include a bit in the conclusion about how he fits into the novel's larger message about childhood, innocence, or family life.

- **Stay relevant.** Your conclusion should suggest new directions of thought, but it shouldn't be treated as an opportunity to pad your essay with all the extra, interesting ideas you came up with during your brainstorming sessions but couldn't fit into the essay proper. Don't attempt to stuff in unrelated queries or too many abstract thoughts.

- **Avoid making overblown closing statements.** A conclusion should open up your highly specific, focused discussion, but it should do so without drawing a sweeping lesson about life or human nature. Making such observations may be part of the point of reading, but it's almost always a mistake in essays, where these observations tend to sound overly dramatic or simply silly.

A+ Essay Checklist

Congratulations! If you've followed all the steps we've outlined, you should have a solid literary essay to show for all your efforts. What if you've got your sights set on an A+? To write the kind of superlative essay that will be rewarded with a perfect grade, keep the following rubric in mind. These are the qualities that teachers expect to see in a truly A+ essay. How does yours stack up?

- ✓ Demonstrates a thorough understanding of the book
- ✓ Presents an original, compelling argument
- ✓ Thoughtfully analyzes the text's formal elements
- ✓ Uses appropriate and insightful examples
- ✓ Structures ideas in a logical and progressive order
- ✓ Demonstrates a mastery of sentence construction, transitions, grammar, spelling, and word choice

Suggested Essay Topics

1. How does Jeannette's relationship with Dad change over the course of the memoir, and why?

2. Dad never starts construction on the Glass Castle he promises to build his family. Why is "The Glass Castle" still an appropriate title for the memoir?

3. Dinitia Hewitt appears briefly and sporadically, but she appears to be Jeannette's only significant childhood friend. In what ways does Dinitia affect Jeannette's development?

4. At the end of the memoir, the family toasts to Dad's life despite all he's put them through. Why are their feelings toward Dad so complicated?

5. Jeannette, Lori, and Brian all forge successful lives for themselves that appear to share little in common with the lives their parents chose. What, if anything, have they taken from their parents and their upbringing?

6. What do the men Jeannette dates reveal about her changing values, and how does her past affect her choices and decisions?

Glossary of Literary Terms

ANTAGONIST

The entity that acts to frustrate the goals of the *protagonist*. The antagonist is usually another *character* but may also be a nonhuman force.

ANTIHERO / ANTIHEROINE

A *protagonist* who is not admirable or who challenges notions of what should be considered admirable.

CHARACTER

A person, animal, or any other thing with a personality that appears in a *narrative*.

CLIMAX

The moment of greatest intensity in a text or the major turning point in the *plot*.

CONFLICT

The central struggle that moves the *plot* forward. The conflict can be the *protagonist*'s struggle against fate, nature, society, or another person.

FIRST-PERSON POINT OF VIEW

A literary style in which the *narrator* tells the story from his or her own *point of view* and refers to himself or herself as "I." The narrator may be an active participant in the story or just an observer.

HERO / HEROINE

The principal *character* in a literary work or *narrative*.

IMAGERY

Language that brings to mind sense-impressions, representing things that can be seen, smelled, heard, tasted, or touched.

MOTIF

A recurring idea, structure, contrast, or device that develops or informs the major *themes* of a work of literature.

NARRATIVE

A story.

LITERARY ANALYSIS

NARRATOR
> The person (sometimes a *character*) who tells a story; the *voice* assumed by the writer. The narrator and the author of the work of literature are not the same thing.

PLOT
> The arrangement of the events in a story, including the sequence in which they are told, the relative emphasis they are given, and the causal connections between events.

POINT OF VIEW
> The *perspective* that a *narrative* takes toward the events it describes.

PROTAGONIST
> The main *character* around whom the story revolves.

SETTING
> The location of a *narrative* in time and space. Setting creates mood or atmosphere.

SUBPLOT
> A secondary *plot* that is of less importance to the overall story but that may serve as a point of contrast or comparison to the main plot.

SYMBOL
> An object, *character*, figure, or color that is used to represent an abstract idea or concept.

SYNTAX
> The way the words in a piece of writing are put together to form lines, phrases, or clauses; the basic structure of a piece of writing.

THEME
> A fundamental and universal idea explored in a literary work.

TONE
> The author's attitude toward the subject or *characters* of a story or poem or toward the reader.

VOICE
> An author's individual way of using language to reflect his or her own personality and attitudes. An author communicates voice through *tone*, *diction*, and *syntax*.

LITERARY ANALYSIS

A NOTE ON PLAGIARISM

Plagiarism—presenting someone else's work as your own—rears its ugly head in many forms. Many students know that copying text without citing it is unacceptable. But some don't realize that even if you're not quoting directly, but instead are paraphrasing or summarizing, it is plagiarism unless you cite the source.

Here are the most common forms of plagiarism:

- Using an author's phrases, sentences, or paragraphs without citing the source

- Paraphrasing an author's ideas without citing the source

- Passing off another student's work as your own

How do you steer clear of plagiarism? You should always acknowledge all words and ideas that aren't your own by using quotation marks around verbatim text or citations like footnotes and endnotes to note another writer's ideas. For more information on how to give credit when credit is due, ask your teacher for guidance or visit www.sparknotes.com.

REVIEW & RESOURCES

QUIZ

1. What is Jeannette doing when she sees Mom on the streets of New York City?

    A. Walking her dog
    B. Sitting in a taxi
    C. Eating dinner with her husband
    D. Taking pictures

2. What is Jeannette doing when her tutu catches fire?

    A. Cooking hot dogs
    B. Playing with matches
    C. Trying to stay warm
    D. Playing with hazardous waste

3.   What does Dad call it when he checks Jeannette out of the
      hospital without paying?

      A.   The ten-finger discount
      B.   Boosting
      C.   Checking out Rex Walls-style
      D.   Sticking it to the man

4.   What does Dad call moving towns in the middle of the night?

      A.   Doing the skedaddle
      B.   Blowing this popsicle stand
      C.   Making like a tree
      D.   Getting out of dodge

5.   Which "star" does Jeannette pick out as her Christmas gift?

      A.   Orion
      B.   Venus
      C.   Bellatrix
      D.   The North Star

6.   What is the Green Lantern?

      A.   A popular bar
      B.   A brothel
      C.   The Walls family's car
      D.   Jeannette's kerosene lamp

7.   What gift does Billy Deel give to Jeannette?

      A.   A silver and turquoise ring
      B.   A book of poems
      C.   Lip gloss
      D.   A car

8.   What job does Mom get to help pay the bills?

      A.   Art instructor
      B.   Jewelry store clerk
      C.   Schoolteacher
      D.   Grocery clerk

9. When does Lori decide she wants to become an artist?

    A. When Mom buys her art supplies
    B. When she gets glasses
    C. When she visits the Grand Canyon
    D. When she meets a famous artist

10. What big request does Jeannette make for her
    tenth birthday?

    A. For Dad to build the Glass Castle
    B. For Dad to stop drinking
    C. For Mom to divorce Dad
    D. To go to New York City

11. What event leads Dinitia and Jeannette to become friends?

    A. Dinitia invites Jeannette to the pool
    B. Jeannette does Dinitia's homework
    C. Jeannette helps Dinitia's neighbor
    D. Jeannette fights Ernie Goad

12. What street do the Wallses move to after leaving Erma's?

    A. Little Hobart Street
    B. Little Beaker Street
    C. Little Armory Street
    D. Little Hollow Street

13. Why is Ginnie Sue Pastor an outcast in Welch?

    A. She is the town prostitute
    B. She is on welfare
    C. She stole from the church
    D. Her son is a murderer

14. Why doesn't Jeannette like to use the neighborhood
    pool in Welch?

    A. She can't afford the entrance fee
    B. She's afraid of water
    C. Bullies hang out there
    D. She is self-conscious

15.   Why does Jeannette join the school paper?

    A.   She wants to be a writer
    B.   It's a free school club
    C.   To interview Chuck Yaeger
    D.   So people will respect her

16.   What does Jeannette steal from the jewelry store and
      then return?

    A.   A diamond ring
    B.   Money from the cash register
    C.   A watch
    D.   A locket for Lori's birthday

17.   What does Dad show Jeannette before she leaves Welch?

    A.   The blueprints for the Glass Castle
    B.   The memoir he is writing
    C.   The money he stole
    D.   Venus at night

18.   What is the name of the Brooklyn newspaper where
      Jeannette has an internship?

    A.   *The Gryffin*
    B.   *The Pyramid*
    C.   *The Phoenix*
    D.   *The Sphinx*

19.   What event causes Jeannette to encourage Maureen to come
      to New York City?

    A.   A neighbor attacks Maureen
    B.   Maureen falls through the stairs
    C.   Dad whips Maureen
    D.   A snake bites Maureen

20.   How much does Dad contribute for Jeannette's tuition
      at Barnard?

    A. $950 and a mink coat
    B.   Nothing
    C. $250 of Lori's waitressing tips
    D. $5,000 from pawning Mom's ring

21. What career does Brian pursue?

    A. Sports writing
    B. Construction
    C. Law enforcement
    D. Soccer coaching

22. How much is Mom's oil-rich property in Texas likely worth?

    A. $500,000
    B. A million dollars
    C. The property never existed
    D. Twenty million dollars

23. What causes Maureen to spend a year in a psychiatric unit?

    A. She lets a cheetah out of its cage at the zoo
    B. She leaps out of a building
    C. She attacks a police officer
    D. She tries to stab Mom

24. How does Dad die?

    A. Tuberculosis
    B. He is attacked outside his apartment
    C. He stumbles in front of a moving car
    D. Heart attack

25. What does Jeannette's husband John think of her scars?

    A. They're ugly
    B. They're tragic
    C. They prove her strength
    D. He doesn't notice them

ANSWER KEY

1. B; 2. A; 3. C; 4. A; 5. B; 6. B; 7. A; 8. C; 9. B; 10. B; 11. C; 12. A; 13. A; 14. C; 15. B; 16. C; 17. A; 18. C; 19. B; 20. A; 21. C; 22. B; 23. D; 24. D; 25. C

REVIEW & RESOURCES

SUGGESTIONS FOR FURTHER READING

Catte, Elizabeth. *What You Are Getting Wrong about Appalachia*. Cleveland, Ohio: Belt Publishing, 2018.

La Ferla, Ruth. *Jeannette Walls Settles Down Far From the Noise of New York*. The New York Times, August 5, 2017. https://www.nytimes.com/2017/08/05/fashion/jeannette-walls-settles-down-far-from-the-noise-of-new-york.html.

Prose, Francine. *'The Glass Castle': Outrageous Misfortune*. The New York Times. March 13, 2005. https://www.nytimes.com/2005/03/13/books/review/the-glass-castle-outrageous-misfortune.html

Walls, Jeannette. *Half Broke Horses: A True-Life Novel*. New York: Scribner, 2009.

Walls, Jeannette. *The Silver Star: A Novel*. New York: Scribner, 2013.

Walls, Jeannette. "How Jeannette Walls Claimed Her Truth." Podcast audio. *Inflection Point with Lauren Schiller*. KALW San Francisco and PRX. August 17, 2017. https://www.salon.com/2017/08/17inside-jeannette-walls-the-glass-castle.

Windolf, Jim. *A Secret of Her Own*. Vanity Fair, April 1, 2005. https://www.vanityfair.com/hollywood/2005/04/jeannette-walls-msnbc-gossip-past.

Witchel, Alex. *How Jeannette Walls Spins Good Stories Out of Bad Memories*. The New York Times Magazine, May 24, 2013. https://www.nytimes.com/2013/05/26/magazine/how-jeannette-walls-spins-good-stories-out-of-bad-memories.html.